TIME
AND THE CONWAYS

A Play in Three Acts

by
J. B. PRIESTLEY

SAMUEL  FRENCH

LONDON
NEW YORK TORONTO SYDNEY HOLLYWOOD

TIME AND THE CONWAYS

Produced at the Duchess Theatre, London, W.C.2, on August 26th, 1937, with the following cast of characters:

CONWAYS: MRS. CONWAY . . . . *Barbara Everest.*

ALAN . . . . *Raymond Huntley.*

MADGE . . . . *Molly Rankin.*

ROBIN . . . . *Alexander Archdale.*

HAZEL . . . . *Rosemary Scott.*

KAY . . . . *Joan Forbes-Robertson.*

CAROL . . . . *Eileen Erskine.*

OTHERS: JOAN HELFORD . . . . *Helen Horsey.*

ERNEST BEEVERS . . . . *Mervyn Johns*

GERALD THORNTON . . . . *Wilfred Babbage.*

The Play produced by IRENE HENTSCHEL.

SYNOPSIS OF SCENES

ACT I.
That night. Kay's twenty-first birthday.

ACT II.
Another night. And another birthday.

ACT III.
That night again. Her twenty-first birthday.
(Act III is continuous with Act I.)

The scene throughout is a sitting-room in Mrs. Conway's house, a detached villa in a prosperous suburb of a manufacturing town, Newlingham. Acts I and III take place on an autumn night in 1919. Act II on an autumn night at the present time.

ACT I. and ACT III.

ACT II.

TIME AND THE CONWAYS*

ACT I

SCENE.—*A sitting-room in* MRS. CONWAY'S *house. An autumn evening of* 1919.

The room looks very cosy, although it has no doorway, only the large curtained archway on the R. *At the back is a window with a step up to it, and a cushioned seat. The curtains are drawn. On the* L. *is a fireplace with an anthracite stove, glowing red. There are several small bookcases against and in the walls, some pieces of fairly good furniture, and some passable pictures. It is obviously one of those nondescript rooms, used by the family far more than the drawing-room is, and variously called the Back Room, the Morning Room, the School Room, the Nursery, the Blue, Brown or Red Room. This might easily have been called the Red Room, for in this light it seems to range from pink to plum colour, and it makes a fine cosy setting for the girls in their party dresses.*

(See Photograph of Scene.)

When the CURTAIN *rises, the stage is in darkness. Then all we can see at first is the strong light from the hall coming gradually up through the curtained archway on the* R. *of the room, and a little red firelight on the other side. But we can hear young voices chattering and laughing and singing, the sharp little explosion of a cracker or two, and a piano playing popular musical-comedy tunes of the period. After a moment, a number of voices begin to sing the tune we hear on the piano. It is all very jolly indeed, and the total effect should be that of a party in progress, which has not yet invaded this room. Plenty of time should be given the audience to take this in before individual voices are distinctly heard.*

HAZEL (*off* R., *but loud and clear*). Mother, where shall we put them ?

MRS. CONWAY (*farther off, but very clear*). In the back room. Then we'll act out here.

HAZEL (*off*). Yes, marvellous ! (*Calling to somebody farther away, almost screaming.*) Carol—in the back room. Don't let them come in, will you, Mother.

(After a moment, she dashes in, switching on the light from the switch below the arch R. *She is a very pretty girl in her very early*

*twenties, nicely dressed in a sort of semi-evening dress. She is
carrying an armful of old clothes, hats, etc., that people use for
charades. She is in high spirits.*

　　By the time HAZEL *has put down—on the ottoman* R.C.—*her
old clothes,* CAROL CONWAY *dashes in with another armful.
CAROL is only about seventeen or eighteen, a very attractive,
sweet-natured, high-spirited girl. Now she is excited—and breathless from dashing up and down stairs. Her stock includes a
cigar-box filled with old false moustaches and beards, false noses,
monocles and spectacles, etc.* HAZEL *switches on the standard
lamp down* L. *from the switch below the arch* R. CAROL *drops
an old lady's felt hat containing a small black fan, red rose and
Spanish comb, on the table up* R.)

CAROL (*panting*).　I've found—(*gasps*)—the box—with all the
false whiskers and things in. (*She puts the rest of her bundle on
the chesterfield* L.)

HAZEL (*triumphantly*).　I knew it hadn't been thrown away.
(*She moves* C.)

CAROL (R. *of the chesterfield*).　Nobody'd dare to throw it away.
(*She holds it out, with the lid open.*)　Look!

　　　　(HAZEL, R. *of* CAROL, *makes a grab at it.*)

Don't *snatch*!

HAZEL (*not angrily*).　Well, I must *look*, mustn't I, idiot?

(*They both, like children, eagerly explore the contents of the box.*)

Bags I this one. (*She fishes out a large drooping black moustache.*)　Oo—and this! (*She fishes out a very bulbous false nose
with red moustache attached.*)

CAROL (*an unselfish creature*).　All right, but don't take *all*
the good ones, Hazel.　Kay and Madge will want some. (*She
crosses to below* L. *end of the chesterfield, looking through the clothes.*)
I think Kay ought to have *first* choice.　After all, it's *her* birthday
—and you know how she adores charades.　Mother won't want
any of these because she'd rather look grand, wouldn't she?
Spanish or Russian or something.　What are you doing?

(HAZEL *has turned aside to fasten on the nose and moustache and
now has managed it, though they are not very secure. She now
turns round.*)

HAZEL (*above the ottoman, in a deep voice*).　Good morning, good
morning.

CAROL (*moving to* L. *of* HAZEL—*with a scream of delight*).　Mr.
Pennyman!　You know, Hazel, at the paper shop?　The one
who hates Lloyd George and wags his head very slowly all the
time he tells you Lloyd George is no good.　Do Mr. Pennyman,
Hazel.　Go on.

HAZEL (*in her ordinary voice, incongruous*). I couldn't, Carol. I've only seen him about twice. I never go to the paper shop.

(ALAN *looks in, grinning when he sees* HAZEL. *He is a shy, quiet young man, in his earlier twenties, who can have a slight stammer. He is dressed rather carelessly in ordinary clothes.* CAROL *sees him. She crosses above* HAZEL *to* ALAN *in the arch, takes his hand and brings him in to* L. *of* HAZEL.)

CAROL. Alan, come in and don't let the others see. Isn't she *exactly* like Mr. Pennyman at the paper shop, the one who hates Lloyd George ?

ALAN (*grinning shyly*). She is—a bit.

HAZEL (*in a fantastic deep voice*). " I hate Lloyd George."

ALAN. No, he doesn't talk like that, Hazel.

CAROL. Not the least little bit. (*She pushes* HAZEL *away to up* R. *and kneels on the upstage seat of the ottoman.*) He says— (*with a rather good imitation of a thick semi-educated man's voice*) " I'll tell yew what it is—Mish Conway—that there Lloyd George— they're going to be shorry they ever put 'im where they did—shee? "

ALAN (*at* R. *end of the chesterfield, grinning*). Yes, that's him. Very good, Carol.

CAROL (*rising—excitedly*). I think I ought to be an actress. They said at school I was the best Shylock they'd ever had.

HAZEL (*taking off the nose and moustache*). You can have these if you like, Carol. (*She comes* C., *to* R. *of* CAROL, *hands them over, then passes on to sit at* L. *end of the chesterfield.*)

CAROL (*taking them*). Are you sure you don't want them ? I don't think you ought to dress up as a silly man, because you're so pretty. Perhaps I could wear these and do Mr. Pennyman. Couldn't we bring him into the third syllable somehow ? Instead of a general. I think we've had enough generals.

ALAN. We have. Ask Kay to work in Mr. Pennyman instead.

HAZEL. Kay ought to be here now, planning everything.

ALAN. She's coming in. Mother told me to tell you not to make too much of a mess in here.

CAROL. You *must* have a mess with charades. It's part of it.

HAZEL. And just wait till Mother starts dressing up. She makes more mess than anybody. (*To* ALAN.) I hope some of the old ones are going now. Are they ?

ALAN. Yes.

HAZEL. It's much more fun without them. And Mother daren't let herself go while they're still here. Tell Kay and Madge to come in, Alan.

ALAN. Right.

(ALAN *goes out. Some voices are heard above the background of party noises, saying, " Are they nearly ready ? " etc. etc. The two girls begin turning the clothes over.* HAZEL *picks out some old-fashioned women's things and holds them up or against herself.*)

HAZEL (*below the chesterfield, picking up an old-fashioned lady's evening cloak*).   Look at this !   Could you believe people *ever* wore such ridiculous things ?

CAROL (*crossing to take it from* HAZEL).   I can just remember Mother in that, can't you ?   (*She returns, looking at it, and puts it down on the upstage seat of the ottoman.*)

HAZEL.   Of course I can, infant !

(*Piano and noises stop.*)

CAROL (*more soberly, looking at a man's old-fashioned shooting or Norfolk coat which she has picked up from the upstage seat of the ottoman*).   That was Daddy's, wasn't it ?

HAZEL.   Yes.   I believe he wore it—that very holiday.

CAROL.   Perhaps we ought to put it away.

HAZEL.   I don't think Mother would mind—now.

CAROL (*holding the coat against herself*).   Yes, she would.   And I know I would.   I don't want anybody to dress up and be funny in the coat Father wore just before he was drowned.   (*A pause. She puts the coat behind the curtain in* R. *corner of the window-seat and turns, standing on the step.*)   I wonder if it's very horrible being drowned.

HAZEL (*impatiently*).   Oh, don't start that all over again, Carol. Don't you remember how you used to go on asking that—until Mother was furious ?

CAROL.   Yes—but I was only a kid then.

HAZEL.   Well, now that you think you aren't a kid any longer, just stop it.

CAROL (*coming down to* R. *end of the chesterfield*).   It was the coat that made me remember.   You see, Hazel, to be talking and laughing and all jolly, all just the same as usual—and then, only half an hour afterwards—to be drowned—it's so horrible. It seemed awfully quick to us—but perhaps to him, there in the water, it may have seemed to take ages——

HAZEL (*crossing below the ottoman to* R. *of it*).   Oh, stop it, Carol.   Just when we're having some fun.   Why do you ?

(*Piano re-starts playing softly "The Tickle Toe"—2nd part chorus 2½ times.*)

CAROL (*coming* C.).   I don't know.   But don't you often feel like that ?   Just when everything is very jolly and exciting, I suddenly think of something awfully serious, sometimes horrible —like Dad drowning—or that little mad boy I once saw with the *huge* head—or that old man who walks in the Park with that great lump growing out of his face——

HAZEL (*stopping her ears*).   I'm not listening.   I'm not listening.

CAROL (L. *of the ottoman*).   They pop up right in the middle of the jolly stuff, you know, Hazel. It happens to Kay too. So it must be in the family—a bit.

(*Some voices are heard off. Enter* MADGE. *She is a year or two older than* HAZEL, *not so pretty, and a far more serious and responsible person. She has been to Girton, and already done a little teaching, and you feel all this in her brisk, decided, self-confident manner. She is too an earnest enthusiast.*)

MADGE (*looking at the things on the ottoman and crossing above it to below the chesterfield, where she picks up a man's old overcoat*). You found them ? Good. I didn't think we'd have so many old things left. Mother ought to have given them away.

(HAZEL *drifts up to the table up* R. CAROL, *who allowed* MADGE *to cross below her, goes to* R. *of the ottoman to look for clothes.*)

HAZEL (*going above the ottoman to the* R. *arm of the chesterfield and sitting*). I'm glad she didn't. Besides, who'd have had them ?

MADGE (*at the fireplace*). Lots of people would have been glad of them. You never realize, Hazel, how wretchedly poor most people are. It just doesn't occur to you, does it ?

HAZEL (*not crossly*). Don't be schoolmistressy, Madge.

(CAROL *has been putting on a mandarin collar at the mirror over the desk down* R. *and now holds a fan behind her head as head-dress.*)

CAROL (*pointing at* MADGE, *impishly*). Has Gerald Thornton arrived ?

MADGE. As a matter of fact, he has—a few minutes ago.

CAROL (*triumphantly*). I knew it. I could see it in your eye, Madge.

(MADGE *runs across at* CAROL *below the ottoman.* CAROL *backs to the desk and throws the fan at her.*)

MADGE. Don't be absurd. (*Going to the table up* R. *and picking up the old felt hat.*) He's brought another man with him, a new client of his, who's desperately anxious to know this family.

HAZEL. So he ought to be. Nice ?

MADGE (*returning to below the chesterfield*). Oh—a funny little man.

CAROL (*above the ottoman, dancing about*). That's just what we want—a funny little man. Perfect for charades.

MADGE. No, not that kind. In fact, he probably hasn't any sense of humour. Very shy, so far, and terrified of Mother. Very much the little business man, I should think.

CAROL. Is he a profiteer—like the ones in " Punch " ?

MADGE. He looks as if he might be, some day. His name's Ernest Beevers.

Hazel (*sliding off the* R. *arm of the chesterfield to sit in* R. *corner of it—giggling*). What a silly name! I'm sorry for his wife, if he has one.

(*The piano stops.*)

Madge. I gather he hasn't. Look here, we ought to be starting.

(*Voices—*"Hurry up, Kay," *etc., stopping with the noise of a door shutting. Enter* Kay, *whose twenty-first birthday party this is. An intelligent, sensitive girl, who need not be as pretty as* Hazel. *She has a sheet of paper and pencil.*)

Kay, we ought to be starting.

Kay (*above the ottoman*). I know. The others are coming. (*She begins rooting among the things.*) Some good costumes, here, laddies. Oo—look! (*She picks out from the upstage seat of the ottoman a large black cloak. She throws it round her, then goes up to the window, stands and strikes an absurd melo-dramatic attitude and speaks in a false stilted tone.*) One moment, Lord Thing-umti-bob. If I am discovered here, who will believe that my purpose in coming here to-night—visiting your—er—rooms—er—unaccompanied—was solely to obtain the—er—papers—that will enable me to clear—er—my husband's name, the name of a man who—er—has asked nothing better than the—er—privilege of serving his country—one who—that is—to whom—— (*Dropping* C. *and speaking in an ordinary tone.*) No, I'm getting all tied up. You know, we ought to have had a scene like that, all grand and dramatic and full of *papers.*

Madge. Well, what *are* we to have ?

Hazel (*coolly*). I've forgotten the word.

(Madge *goes up* L. *of the chesterfield, gets "The Nation" from the table behind the chesterfield and some feathers to adorn her hat. She then drifts back at her leisure to sit on the footstool by the fire* L., *fixing the feathers and glancing at "The Nation."*)

Carol (*above the ottoman, indignantly*). Hazel, you're the *limit*! And we spent hours working it out !

Hazel. I didn't. Only you and Kay, just because you fancy yourselves as budding authoresses and actresses.

Kay (R. *of the chesterfield, severely*). The word—idiot !—is *Pussyfoot.* Puss. See. Foot. Then the whole word.

Madge. I think four scenes are too many. And they'll easily guess it.

Kay. That doesn't matter. It makes them happy if they guess it.

Carol (*rather solemnly*). The great thing is—to *dress up.*

(*Voices—*"Can't we go in yet ? Do let me see," *etc. Enter* Mrs. Conway. *She is a charming woman in her middle forties, very nicely dressed, with an easy vivacious manner.*)

MRS. CONWAY. Now I'm ready—if you are. (*She comes to above the ottoman, throwing things about as she looks for something.*) What a mess you're making. I knew you would. Let me see.

(*She dives further into the clothes, and scatters them far more wildly than the others have done. Crossing to below the chesterfield she finally fishes out a Spanish shawl.*)

Ah—here they are. Now, I shall be a Spanish beauty. (*Moving to* C.) I know a song for it, too. (*She begins putting the Spanish things on.*)

(KAY *fetches safety-pins from the table up* R. *and comes back to* L. *of her.* CAROL *assists from* R. *of her.*)

HAZEL (*to* KAY). What did I tell you ?

MRS. CONWAY (*who is specially fond of* HAZEL). What did you tell her, darling ?

HAZEL. I told Kay, whatever she arranged, you'd insist on doing your Spanish turn.

MRS. CONWAY. Well, why not ?

KAY. It doesn't come into the scenes I'd thought of, that's all.

MRS. CONWAY (*busy with her costume*). Oh—you can easily arrange that, dear—you're so clever. I've just been telling Doctor Halliday and his niece how clever you are. They seemed surprised, I can't imagine why.

(*She goes to the table up* R. *for the fan, comb and rose.* CAROL *helps her.*)

HAZEL. It's the first time I've seen Monica Halliday out of her land-girl costume. I'm surprised she didn't turn up to-night in her trousers and leggings.

(MRS. CONWAY *comes down to the mirror above the desk down* R. *to fix her Spanish comb, then throws the lace collar of her frock over it for a mantilla.* CAROL *stands on the* R. *seat of the ottoman to help.*)

KAY. She looks quite queer out of them, doesn't she ? Rather like a female impersonator.

MADGE. Oh, come on, Kay. What do we do ?

KAY. The first scene, *Puss*, is an old lady who's lost her cat. She's really a kind of witch.

CAROL (*happily, jumping off the ottoman and going above it*). I'm to be the old lady.

(*She begins finding suitable clothes—a black skirt, an old shawl with some white hair attached for the old lady. During the following dialogue, she converts herself into a very creditable imitation.*)

KAY. Mother, you and Hazel are her two daughters who are visiting her——

MRS. CONWAY (*still adjusting her get-up at the mirror*). Yes, dear.

HAZEL. I know my bit. I keep saying, " I always hated that terrible cat of yours, Mother." What can I wear ? (*She pokes about.*)

MRS. CONWAY (*crossing below the ottoman to* L.C., *below the chesterfield—now Spanish*). Well, that's all right, dear, I'll be the Spanish daughter, you see.

KAY (*at* R. *end of the chesterfield, resignedly*). She didn't have a Spanish daughter, but I suppose it doesn't matter.

MRS. CONWAY (*sitting in* R. *corner of the chesterfield*). Not in the least. Nobody cares. And then I think I'd better not appear in the others, because I suppose you'll be wanting me to sing afterwards.

KAY. Of course. But I'd put you down for two more. Madge and Joan Helford will have to do those.

(*During the following scene* CAROL *sits on* R. *seat of the ottoman and* HAZEL *on upstage seat of ottoman, very unobtrusively arranging their costumes.* MADGE *is sitting on the footstool by the fire* L., *reading " The Nation."*)

MRS. CONWAY. What a pity Robin isn't here ! You know, Madge, he wrote and said he might be demobbed any day now, and it seems such a shame just to miss Kay's party. Robin loves parties. He's like me. Your father never cared for them much. Suddenly, right in the middle, just when everything was getting going, he'd want to be quiet—and take me into a corner and ask me how much longer people were staying—just when they were beginning to enjoy themselves. I never could understand that.

KAY. I can. I've often felt like that.

MRS. CONWAY. But why, dear, why ? It isn't sensible. If you're having a party, you're having a party.

KAY (*earnestly*). Yes, it isn't that. And it isn't that you suddenly dislike the people. But you feel—at least I do, and I suppose that's what Father felt too—you feel, quite suddenly, that it isn't *real* enough—and you want something to be *real*. Do you see, Mother ?

MRS. CONWAY. No, I don't, my dear. It sounds a little morbid to me. But your father could be quite morbid sometimes—you mightn't think so, but he could—and I suppose you take after him.

KAY (*kneeling* R. *of the chesterfield and speaking very gravely*). Do you think that sometimes, in a mysterious sort of way, he *knew* ?

(HAZEL *has risen to show* CAROL *the evening cloak she is wearing.*)

MRS. CONWAY (*not too attentive to this*). Knew *what*, dear ?
Look at Hazel ; doesn't she look rather sweet ? I can remember
where I first wore those things. Absurd ! Knew *what* ?

(HAZEL *sits again*.)

KAY. Knew what was going to happen to him. You know,
Alan said that some of the men he knew who were killed in the
trenches seemed to know sometimes that they were going to
be killed, as if a kind of shadow fell over them. Just as if—
now and then—we could see round the corner—into the future.

MRS. CONWAY (*easily*). You have the most extraordinary
ideas. You must try and put some of them into your book.
Are you happy, darling ?

KAY (*rising*). Yes, Mother. Very happy.

MRS. CONWAY. That's all right, then. I want you to have a
lovely birthday. I feel we all can be happy again, now that
the horrible war's all over and people are sensible again, and
Robin and Alan are quite safe. I forgot to ask—Did Robin
send you anything, Kay ?

KAY. No. I didn't expect him to.

MRS. CONWAY. Oh—but that isn't like Robin, you know,
Kay. He's a most generous boy, much too generous, really.
Now, that may mean he thinks he's coming home very soon.

Voices off—" Aren't they ready," *etc.,—and continue as back-
ground until cue. Enter* ALAN *with* JOAN HELFORD, *who is*
HAZEL'S *friend and the same age, pretty and rather foolish.*
ALAN *remains by the arch.* JOAN *comes above the ottoman to* ᴄ.)

KAY. Alan, tell them we're beginning—and it's three syllables.

(ALAN *goes.* CAROL *rises and gets her old lady costume ready.*)

JOAN. I think you all look marvellous. I'm rotten at this,
you know, Kay. Don't say I didn't warn you.

KAY. Now then, Carol, you start. And remember, only say
" Puss," once. Don't you two say it—only Carol.

(ALAN *re-enters to downstage corner of arch.* CAROL *puts on her
shawl with grey hair attached and, bent nearly double as the old
lady, goes below and round the ottoman and off, saying :* " Now
where are my two daughters ? Where are they ! I haven't
seen them for years ! " *Loud applause and laughter off as she
exits.*)

Good old Carol ! Now then—you two. (*She almost pushes them
off.*)

(HAZEL *flounces off, followed by* MRS. CONWAY *with exaggerated
Spanish gait. More applause and laughter, which stops with
a door-slam.*)

Now the next syllable is " *S-Y*." So I thought it wouldn't be

cheating too badly if we called that " sy." Y'know, Cockney—
" I sy, Bert." So this is an East End scene. Madge, you're
the old mother.

MADGE (*who has started putting on very droll and shabby clothes—
at the fire*). Yes, I remembered.

ALAN (*above desk* R.) What am I ? I forget.

KAY. You're Bert. Just put something silly on. (*Coming
to above the ottoman.*) Is there anything here you can wear,
Joan ?

(ALAN *drifts across at back to behind chesterfield where he finds a
paper top-hat and scarf.* JOAN, L. *of the ottoman, finds a white
petticoat and starts putting it on.*)

JOAN. I was in London last week, staying with my uncle,
and we went to the theatre *three times.* (*Moving to the table above
the chesterfield and then back to* R. *of the chesterfield.*) We saw
" Tilly of Bloomsbury " and " Cinderella Man " and "Kissing
Time." I liked " Cinderella Man " best——Owen Nares, y'know.
I thought Robin was coming home soon.

KAY (L. *of* JOAN). He is.

JOAN. He's an officer, isn't he ? You weren't an officer,
were you, Alan ?

ALAN (*sitting on the desk down* R.). No, I was a lance-corporal.
One stripe, y'know. Nothing at all.

JOAN. Didn't you want to be anything better than that ?

ALAN. No.

KAY. Alan has no ambition at all. Have you, my pet ?

ALAN (*simply*). Not much.

JOAN. If I were a man, I'd want to be very important.
What are you doing now, Alan ? Somebody said you were at
the Town Hall.

ALAN. I am. In the Rate Office. Just a clerk, y'know.

JOAN. Isn't it dull ?

ALAN. Yes. (*He strikes a match to light his pipe which he has
been filling.*)

KAY. Alan never minds being dull. I believe he has tremendous long adventures inside his head that nobody knows anything about.

JOAN. Hazel says you've started to write another novel, Kay.
Have you ?

KAY (*rather curtly*). Yes.

JOAN. I don't know how you can—I mean, I think I'd be
all right once I'd started properly—but I can't see how you
start. What did you do with the last one ?

KAY. Burnt it.

JOAN. Why ?

KAY. It was putrid.

JOAN. But wasn't that an awful waste of time ?

KAY. Yes, I suppose so.

ALAN. Still, look at the time you and I waste, Joan.

JOAN. Oh—no—I'm always doing *something*. Even though I haven't to go to the canteen any more, I'm always busy.

(MADGE, *still sitting on the footstool by the fire, now laughs.*)

Why do you laugh, Madge ?

MADGE. Can't a girl laugh ?

JOAN (*humbly*). You always did laugh at me, Madge. I suppose because I'm not clever, like you.

(*Voices off and applause, as* HAZEL *enters, then the voice of* MRS. CONWAY *singing* " *Carmen* " [2nd Number—Castanet Dance— Act II].)

HAZEL (*coming to above the ottoman to take off her cloak, etc.*). Well, you can imagine what happened. Mother let herself go, and of course it became all Spanish. I don't believe they'll ever remember hearing " puss " mentioned. What are you supposed to be, Joan ?

JOAN (*below the chesterfield* L.C., *turning round to show her costume*). A sort of coster girl.

HAZEL. You look a sort of general mess. Oh—(*to* Kay) Carol wants to do Mr. Pennyman at the paper shop instead of a general for the third syllable. (*She goes down to the desk* R. *to take the scarf off her head at the mirror.*)

KAY. How can she ? If it's soldiers drilling, you can't have Mr. Pennyman. Unless we make him another soldier—and get Gerald Thornton or somebody to be a general.

(*Loud applause off.* MRS. CONWAY *has finished her song and can now be heard dancing to the repeat of the chorus.* CAROL *returns, very hot and flushed, and begins taking off her old woman's disguise.*)

CAROL (*coming to above the ottoman*). Mother's still on. Golly ! —it's baking being an old witch.

KAY (R. *of the chesterfield*). Do you insist on being Mr. Pennyman in the third syllable ?

CAROL (*brightening up*). Oo—I'd forgotten that. (*To* KAY, *putting her arms round her and swinging her round.*) Yes, please let me do Mr. Pennyman, Kay—my lamb, my love, my precious —— (*After swinging* KAY *round she goes to below the chesterfield.*)

KAY. All right. But he'll have to be a soldier. Just joined up, you see.

(*Big applause and laughter off.* Enter MRS. CONWAY *very grand, flushed, triumphant. She is carrying a glass of claret cup. She comes above the ottoman and sits on* L. *seat of it.*)

MRS. CONWAY. Well—really—that was *very* silly—but they

seemed to enjoy it, and that's the great thing. I thought you
were very good, Carol. (*To* KAY.) Carol was sweet, Kay.
Now, don't ask me to do any more of this, because really I
mustn't, especially if you want me to sing afterwards. So leave
me out, Kay. (*She begins to sip cup.*)

KAY. All right. Now, come on——

(*She begins shepherding her players,* MADGE, ALAN, JOAN.)

JOAN. Honestly, Kay, I'll be *awful*——

KAY. It doesn't matter. You've nothing to do. Now then—
Madge——

MADGE (*loudly, in laborious imitation of a Cockney mother*).
Nah then, Bert. End yew, Dy-sy. Cem along or we'll be lite.

(*She crosses above the ottoman to the arch and, taking* JOAN *and*
ALAN *with her, leads the way off. Applause, and then voices
finish on door-slam.*)

HAZEL (R. *of the ottoman*). How on earth did you get that
claret cup, Mother ?

MRS. CONWAY (*complacently*). Got Gerald Thornton to hand
it to me—and it rounded off my little scene nicely. I don't
want any more. Would you like it ?

(HAZEL *takes it and sips. They are all removing things.*)

CAROL (*having now put on a frock-coat ready for Mr. Pennyman*).
Mother, you weren't going to be an *actress*, were you—just a
singer ? (*She comes to* L. *of* MRS. CONWAY *on the ottoman and
pulls out a pair of trousers on which* MRS. CONWAY *is sitting. She
then goes to below the chesterfield.*)

MRS. CONWAY. I don't know what you mean by *just* a singer.
I was a singer certainly. But I did some acting too. When the
Newlingham Amateur Operatic first did " Merrie England," I
played Bess. And I'd had all you children then. *You* were
only about two, Carol.

HAZEL (*kneeling on* R. *seat of the ottoman*). Mother, Joan *did*
stay in London last week, and she went to three theatres.

MRS. CONWAY. She has relatives there, and we haven't.
That makes a great difference.

HAZEL. Aren't we *ever* going ?

MRS. CONWAY. Yes, of course. Perhaps Robin will take
us—I mean, just you and me—when he comes back——

CAROL (*now kneeling in* R. *corner of chesterfield sorting out her
next props—solemnly*). It says in the paper this morning that
We Must All Get On With Our Jobs. This Mere Rush For
Amusement has gone on long enough now. There's Work
Waiting To Be Done.

HAZEL (*indignantly*). A fat lot of rushing for amusement
we've done, haven't we ? I think that's frightfully unfair and

idiotic. Just when we *might* have some fun, after washing up in canteens and hospitals and queueing for foul food, with *nobody* about at all, they go and say we've had enough amusement and must get on with our jobs. What jobs ?

CAROL (*getting off the chesterfield to pull on her trousers for " Mr. Pennyman)"*. Re-building a shattered world. It said that too.

MRS. CONWAY (*half lightly, half not, to* HAZEL). Your job will be to find a very nice young man and marry him. And *that* oughtn't to be difficult—for you.

CAROL. Hurry up, Hazel, and then I can be a bridesmaid. I believe you're my *only* chance. Kay says she won't get married for *ages*, if ever, because her Writing—her Work—must come first. (*She puts a large pad—a dress folded up—into her trousers for " Mr. Pennyman's " stomach.*)

MRS. CONWAY. That's nonsense, my dear. When the right young man comes along, she'll forget about her writing.

CAROL. I don't believe she will, Mother. And anyhow, she won't have bridesmaids. (*She goes up* R. *of the chesterfield with her back to the audience, getting moustache, etc., from the table above it.*) And if Madge ever marries, I know it will be to some kind of Socialist in a tweed suit, who'll insist on being married in a Registry Office——

HAZEL. I'm not so sure about that. I've had my eye on Madge lately.

CAROL (*turning by* R. *end of chesterfield as " Mr. Pennyman "—bowler-hat, glasses, walrus moustache, old morning coat and check trousers*). And I've 'ad my eye on Lloyd George. (*With a gesture to command attention.*) An' what for, Mish Conway ? Bee-corsh yew can't trusht that little Welshman. Yew watch 'im, that'sh all I shay—yew watch 'im !

MRS. CONWAY. That's *very* good, dear. You're rather like Mr. Worsnop—do you remember him—the cashier at the works ? Every New Year's Eve your father used to bring Mr. Worsnop here, after they'd done all the books at the office, and used to give him some port. And when I went in, Mr. Worsnop always stood and held his glass like this (*she holds an imaginary glass in a rather cringing attitude*) and say " My respects, Mrs. Conway, my deepest respects." And I always wanted to laugh. He's retired now, and gone to live in South Devon. (*She rises and goes below the ottoman to the desk down* R.)

(*After a slight pause,* MADGE, *still in her absurd old costerwoman disguise, enters, followed by* GERALD THORNTON. *He is in his early thirties, a solicitor and son of a solicitor, and is fairly tall and good-looking, and carefully dressed. He has a pleasant, man-of-the-world air, very consciously cultivated.* MADGE *is arguing hotly, with all the fiery slapdash of enthusiastic youth.*)

MADGE. That's perfectly true, Gerald. (*As she enters.*) But what the miners want and ask for is simply nationalization.

(*She comes above the ottoman to below the chesterfield.* GERALD *follows to* R. *of her.* CAROL *and* HAZEL *go to the table up* R. *for chocolates and give one to* MRS. CONWAY.)

They say, if coal is so important as you say it is, then the mines shouldn't be in the hands of private owners any longer. Nationalize them, they say. That's the fairest thing.

GERALD. All right. But supposing we don't want them nationalized. What then? Some of us have seen enough of government mismanagement already.

MRS. CONWAY (R. *of the ottoman with chocolate*). Quite so, Gerald. Everybody knows how ridiculous they were. Sending bags of sand to Egypt!

MADGE (*crossing to above the ottoman, taking off coster costume—hotly*). I don't believe half those stories. Besides, they had to improvise everything in a hurry. And anyhow, it wasn't a *Socialist* government.

GERALD (*mildly*). But you don't know they'd be any better. They might be worse—less experience.

MADGE (*in the same tone*). Oh—I know that *experience*! We're always having that flung in our faces. When all that's wanted is a little intelligence—and enthusiasm—and—and decency.

(*Voices, etc., off.* MADGE *goes above the chesterfield to put down some of her things.*)

GERALD (*crossing* C. *to* MRS. CONWAY *and speaking rather as one adult to another at a children's party*). I've been conscripted for the next scene. To be a general or something.

HAZEL (*below the table up* R.). We haven't fancy dress for you.

GERALD. Good!

MRS. CONWAY. I really mustn't neglect them any longer, must I? And most of them will be going soon. Then we can have a nice cosy little party of our own.

(*She goes up to the arch and caresses* HAZEL'S *hair as she goes out.*)

CAROL (*moving to* R. *of* GERALD, *who is* C.). Well, you must look different somehow, you know. You could turn your coat inside out. (*She starts to take his coat off.*)

GERALD. I don't think that would be very effective.

CAROL (*impatiently*). Wear an overcoat, then. (*Crossing below him to the chesterfield and kneeling on it.*) Oh—and——
(*She fishes out a large false moustache from the box on the table above the chesterfield and gives it to him.*) Put this on, and this. (*She*

gives him a peaked paper hat.)   That's a *very* good one.   Try them on over there by the mirror.

(CAROL *pushes him down below the ottoman to the mirror above the desk* R.   MADGE *says,* " Here, Gerald," *as she throws a man's overcoat across to him.*   JOAN *rushes in, more animated now her ordeal is over, and comes above the ottoman to* C.)

JOAN (*excitedly, girlish*).   Hazel, d'you know who's here ? You'll never guess !

HAZEL.   Who ?

JOAN.   That *awful* little man who always stares at you—the one who followed us once all round the Park——

HAZEL.   He's *not*!

JOAN.   He is, I tell you.   I distinctly saw him, standing at the side, near the door.

GERALD.   This sounds like my friend Beevers.

HAZEL (*kneeling on the upstage seat of the ottoman*).   Do you mean to say the man you brought is *that* awful little man ?   Well, you're the absolute limit, Gerald Thornton !   He's a *dreadful* little creature.   Every time I go out, he's somewhere about, staring and staring at me.   And now you bring him here !

GERALD (*at the desk down* R., *not worried by this outburst*).   Oh— he's not so bad.   He insisted on my bringing him, and your mother said it was all right.   You shouldn't be so devastating, Hazel.

(JOAN *kneels on the upstage seat of the ottoman,* L. *of* HAZEL. CAROL *kneels on the* L. *seat of the ottoman.*)

JOAN (*giggly*).   I told you he must be mad about you, Hazel.

HAZEL (*the haughty beauty now*).   I swear I won't speak to him.   He just would butt in like this !

CAROL.   Why shouldn't he, poor little manny ?

HAZEL.   Shut up, Carol, you don't know anything about him.

(CAROL *rises and crosses to below the chesterfield, putting on her bowler-hat.   Half-hearted applause off.   Enter* KAY *and* ALAN. KAY *comes* C.   ALAN *joins* CAROL *below the chesterfield.*)

KAY.   That wasn't much good.   The costers were a washout. Oh—that's all right, Carol.   Now, you're a general, Gerald, and the others are recruits.   Hurry up, Alan, and put something different on.   Gerald, you're inspecting them—you know, make up something silly—and then say to one of them, " Look at your *foot*, my man."   Anyhow, bring in " foot."

GERALD (*crossing* L. *to join* CAROL *and* ALAN *below the chesterfield*).   Have I only two recruits, Carol and Alan ?

KAY (C.).   No, mother's sending in another man.   They aren't guessing anything yet, but that's simply because it's all such a muddle.   I don't think I like charades as much as I used to do. Dad was marvellous at them. (*To* GERALD.) He always did very fat men. You'd better be a fat general. And you can be fat too, Alan.

(GERALD *gets two cushions from the chesterfield and* ALAN *one cushion from the chair below the fire. As the men are stuffing cushions under their coats,* ERNEST BEEVERS *enters slowly and shyly. He is a little man, about thirty, still socially shy and awkward, chiefly because his social background is rather lower in the scale than that of the* CONWAYS, *but there is a suggestion of growing force and self-confidence in him. He is obviously attracted towards the whole family, but completely fascinated by* HAZEL.)

ERNEST (*in the archway, shyly and awkwardly*). Oh—er—Mrs. Conway told me to come in here.

(JOAN, *who is sitting on the upstage seat of the ottoman, giggles.* KAY *nudges her to stop her.*)

KAY. Yes, of course. You've to be one of the recruits in this next bit.

ERNEST. I'm—not much good—at this sort of thing—you know——

KAY. It doesn't matter. Just be silly.

GERALD. Oh—Beevers—sorry! (*He turns to reveal his exaggeratedly padded stomach.*) I'd better introduce you.

(*He comes* C., *to* L. *of* BEEVERS. HAZEL *rises and goes down to the desk* R. GERALD *carries off a slightly awkward situation with a determined light touch.*)

This—is Mr. Ernest Beevers, a rather recent arrival in our—er—progressive city. Now, all these are Conways, except this young lady—Miss Joan Helford——

ERNEST (*seriously, shaking hands with her*). How d'you do ?

JOAN (*rising and going down* R. *to join* HAZEL *by the desk—faintly giggly*). How d'you do ?

GERALD. This is Kay, who decided to be twenty-one to-day so that we could have this party——

ERNEST (*crossing to her* C. *to shake hands*). Many happy returns.

KAY (*nicely*). Thank you.

GERALD. She's the literary genius of this distinguished family. Over there is Madge, who's been to Girton and will try to convert you to Socialism.

ERNEST. I'm afraid she won't succeed.

GERALD. This strange-looking middle-aged person is young Carol——

CAROL (*nicely*). Hello ! (*She pulls her moustache off and crosses to* L. *of him to shake hands.*)

ERNEST (*grateful for this, smiling*). Hello !

GERALD. Alan, I think you've met already. (*Teasing.*) Oh—and let me see—yes, this is Hazel. She creates such havoc that when the Leicesters were stationed here, the Colonel wrote and asked her to stay indoors the days when they had route marches.

ERNEST (*moving down* o.—*solemnly*). How d'you do ?

(JOAN *gives* HAZEL *a push forward.*)

HAZEL (*crossly.*) Don't be idiotic, Gerald. (*Very quickly to* ERNEST.) How d'you do ? (*She shakes hands very perfunctorily and returns to* JOAN *at the desk down* R.)

(*There is a faint giggle from* JOAN.)

ALAN (*taking* ERNEST *by the arm and bringing him from down* o. *to below the chesterfield*). You'd better do something funny to yourself. Is there anything here you'd like ?

(ERNEST *pokes about in the things, while* HAZEL *looks disdainfully on and* JOAN *wants to giggle.* ERNEST *is very clumsy now.*)

KAY. Carol and Alan, you start. You're recruits. Carol can do bits of Mr. Pennyman to fill in.

(CAROL, *followed by* ALAN, *marches off.* CAROL *is singing "It's a long way to Tipperary."* KAY *follows them off. Laughs off.*)

JOAN (*sitting on the desk down* R., *above* HAZEL). What did your mother say, Hazel, about removing ?

HAZEL (*sitting on the stool at the desk down* R.). Oh, of course she won't think of it. And she's been offered five thousand pounds—*five thousand*—for this house !

(ERNEST *drops down* L.C. *wearing a lady's felt hat.*)

ERNEST (*the business man*). Miss Conway, tell her to take it. I'll bet in ten years she couldn't get two thousand. It's only this temporary shortage that's forced prices of property up. You'll see 'em come down with a bang yet.

HAZEL (*snubbing him*). But she adores being here, of course, and so it's hopeless.

(ERNEST *realizes he has been snubbed. He looks hard at* HAZEL, *who will not return his look.* JOAN *is still giggly.*)

ERNEST (*with dignity which ill assorts with his appearance*). If I spoke out of my turn, I'm sorry.

(KAY *re-enters and comes up* o.)

KAY. Hurry up, Mr. Beevers.

ERNEST (*hurrying forward*). I'm no good at this, you know,

Miss Conway (*he turns to look at* GERALD *and sees his enormous stomach*), and it's no use pretending I am——

(*He has disappeared with* KAY *and followed by* GERALD THORNTON. *At this moment,* JOAN *bursts into a peal of laughter as she goes up to the* R *end of the chesterfield.*)

HAZEL (*indignantly, going up to the archway*). I don't think it's funny, Joan. I'm *furious*.

JOAN (*between gurgles and gasps*). He—looked—so—silly——

(*She sits at* R. *end of the chesterfield.* HAZEL *begins laughing too and they laugh together, rocking round.*)

HAZEL (*crossing to* R. *end of the chesterfield—hardly distinguishable*). Did you hear him ? " If I spoke out of my turn, I'm sorry."

JOAN (*hardly distinguishable*). We ought to have said " Pleased to meet you " and then he'd have said " Granted."

(KAY *comes back, and looks rather severely at these two.*)

KAY (*at the arch, severely*). I think you were rather beastly to that little man.

(*They still laugh, and as she looks at them* KAY *begins to laugh too. They all laugh.*)

HAZEL (*coming to*). Oh—dear ! Oh—dear ! But that's the little man I told you about, Kay, who always stared, and once followed us round.

KAY (*above the ottoman*). Well, now he'll be able to raise his little hat.

HAZEL (*vehemently*). And that's all he'll jolly well get out of this, I'll tell you. And I think Gerald Thornton had the cheek of the devil to bring him here. Just because he's a new client.

JOAN (*still giggly*). You don't think you'll marry him, then, Hazel ?

HAZEL (*sitting on* R. *arm of the chesterfield*). Ugh ! I'd just as soon marry a—a ferret.

KAY (*rather loftily*). I don't believe you two ever think or talk about anything but clothes and going to London and getting married !

HAZEL (*not too rudely*). Oh, don't you start being so grand ! (*Quoting dramatically.*) " The Garden of Stars ! "

KAY (*hastily*). Now, shut up, Hazel !

HAZEL (*to* JOAN). " The Garden of Stars." That's what she called the last novel she started. And there were so many bits of paper with the opening words on that I know them off by heart. (*She quotes dramatically.*) " Marion went out into the still smooth night."

(KAY *makes a rush at her, but she dodges below the ottoman to* R. *of it, still quoting. They continue to dodge, and* HAZEL *should finish up kneeling* R. *of the ottoman—*KAY L. *of it.*)

"There was no moon, but already—already—the sky was silver-dusted with stars. She passed through the rose garden, the dying scent of the roses meeting the grey moths——"

KAY (*shouting her down*). I know it's all wrong, but I tore it up, didn't I?

HAZEL (*mildly*). Yes, my duck. And then you cried.

KAY (*fiercely*). I've just begun a real one. With some *guts* in it. You'll see.

HAZEL. I'll bet it's about a girl who lives in a town just like Newlingham.

KAY (*still fierce*). Well, why shouldn't it be? You wait, that's all.

(*Voices and laughter off.* GERALD, *plus false moustache,* ALAN *and* ERNEST *in their absurd get-up come in slowly and solemnly.*)

GERALD (*as he enters*). That's quite true, Alan.

(*They cross above the ottoman and form a group* L. *below the chesterfield.* HAZEL *sits on the* R. *seat of the ottoman as the men enter, and* JOAN *rises.*)

ERNEST (*seriously*). They can't expect people to behave differently when they've still got their war restrictions on everything. They can't have it both ways.

GERALD. Well, there's still a lot of profiteering.

ERNEST. You've got to let business find its own level. The more interference the worse it is.

ALAN. The worse for everybody?

ERNEST (*decidedly*). Yes.

ALAN (*stoutly, for him*). I doubt it.

ERNEST (*not too unpleasantly*). You're working in the Town Hall, aren't you? Well, you can't learn much about these things there, y'know.

KAY (*below the ottoman, with tremendous irony*). I say, you three must have been terribly good in the charade, weren't you?

ALAN. No, we weren't very amusing.

CAROL (*who has just entered and crossed above the ottoman to* R. *of* BEEVERS). Oh—they were awful. No, you weren't *too* bad, Mr. Beevers, especially for a man who was doing a charade in a strange house.

(ALAN *and* GERALD *go round* L. *end of the chesterfield to above it as they remove their things.*)

ERNEST. Now, I call that handsome, Miss Carol.

KAY (*at the downstage corner of the arch—briskly*). The whole word now. *Pussyfoot.* It's supposed to be a party in America, and we can't have anything to drink. We won't bother dressing up for this. Just some good *acting*. I'll say the word. Joan, tell Madge, she's in this. Just the girls, for the grand finale.

(JOAN *goes*.)

GERALD (*now normal again*). So we're sacked ?
KAY. Yes. No good.
GERALD (*crossing to the arch*). Then we can give ourselves a drink. We've earned a drink. (*Stopping in the archway.*) Any dancing afterwards ?
KAY. There might be, after Mother's done her singing.
GERALD. Do you dance, Beevers ?
ERNEST (*moving* C.). No, never had time for it.
HAZEL (*significantly, in a loud clear tone*). Yes, we *must* have some dancing, Gerald.
GERALD. Are you coming, Alan ?

(*He goes off, followed by* ALAN. *Voices off—*" Have a drink," *etc. Clink of glasses.* ERNEST *looks hard at* HAZEL. *She gives him a wide innocent stare of complete indifference. He nods, turns and goes.* CAROL *is busy getting out of her Mr. Pennyman disguise.* HAZEL *crosses to below the chesterfield to start collecting clothes.*)

CAROL (*at* R. *end of the chesterfield, excitedly*). Kay, we could have done the Prince of Wales in America for this last scene. Why didn't we think of it ? You could be the Prince of Wales, and you could fall in love with Hazel, who could turn out to be Pussyfoot's daughter.
KAY (*laughing*). Mother'd be shocked. And so would some of the others.
CAROL. I'd hate to be a Prince of Wales, wouldn't you ?
HAZEL (*with decision*). I'd *love* it.
CAROL. Old Mrs. Ferguson—you know, the one with the queer eye—the rather frightening one—told me there was an old prophecy that when King David came to the throne of Britain, everything would be *wonderful*.

(*There is the sound off of a loud shout,* " Robin ! Don't go, Robin ", *etc., then confused voices and laughter.*)

KAY. What's that ?
HAZEL (*excitedly*). It's Robin.

(*They all look up with eager interest.* HAZEL *has gathered up a bundle of clothes. She dashes across, throws them on the chair* L. *of the table up* R. *and meets* ROBIN *in the archway. He is twenty-three, and a rather dashing, good-looking young man in the uniform of an R.A.F. officer. He is in tremendous spirits. He carries a small package in his pocket.*)

ROBIN (*loudly*). Hello, kids ! Hazel ! (*He kisses her, then crosses below her to* KAY, *who is by* R. *end of the chesterfield.*) Kay, many happies ! (*He kisses her, then crosses below her to* CAROL, *who is below the chesterfield.*) Carol, my old hearty ! (*He kisses her, picks her up and spins round with her.*) Gosh ! I've had a dash to get here in time. Did half the journey on one of our lorries. And I didn't forget the occasion, Kay. What about that ?

(*He gives her the parcel from his pocket, which she opens and finds is a silk scarf.*)

All right, isn't it ?

KAY (*gratefully*). It's lovely, Robin. Lovely, lovely ! (*She goes to the desk down* R. *to try it on at the mirror.*)

ROBIN (*sitting on the* R. *arm of the chesterfield*). That's the stuff to give 'em. And I've finished. Out ! Demobbed at last !

HAZEL (R. *of him*). Oo—grand ! Have you seen Mother ?

(CAROL *has jumped on to the chesterfield and is standing on it,* L. *of* ROBIN.)

ROBIN. Of course I have, you chump. You ought to have seen her face when I told her I was now a civilian again. Golly ! we'll have some fun now, won't we ?

KAY. Lots and lots.

CAROL. Have you seen Alan ?

ROBIN. Just for a second. Still the solemn old bird, isn't he ?

CAROL (*very young and solemn*). In my opinion, Alan is a very wonderful person.

ROBIN (*rattling on*). I know. You always thought that, didn't you ? Can't quite see it myself, but I'm very fond of the old crawler. How's the writing, Kay ?

KAY (*sitting on the stool at the desk down* R.). I'm still trying —and learning.

ROBIN. That's the stuff. We'll show 'em. This is where the Conways really begin. How many young men, Hazel ?

HAZEL (*calmly*). Nobody to speak of. (*She moves away a little towards* R., *but* ROBIN *takes her hand and stops her.*)

CAROL. She'd worked her way up to Colonels, hadn't you, Haze ?

KAY (*affectionately*). Now that it's civilians, she's having to change her technique—and she's a bit uncertain yet.

ROBIN. All jealousy that, isn't it, Hazel ?

(*Voices off. One voice can be humming, " It's a long, long trail a-winding." MRS. CONWAY appears in the archway, carrying a tray laden with sandwiches, cake, etc., and a bottle of beer.*)

A-ha, here we are !

(*He rushes to take the tray from her.* MRS. CONWAY *is very happy now.* CAROL *goes to behind the chesterfield to collect some things.* ROBIN *brings the tray with him and sits* L. *on the chesterfield.* MRS. CONWAY *crosses to sit* R. *on the chesterfield beside* ROBIN.)

MRS. CONWAY (*beaming*). Isn't this nice ? Now we're *all* here. I knew somehow you were on your way, Robin, even though you didn't tell us—you naughty boy.

ROBIN. Couldn't, Mother, honestly. Only wangled it at the last minute.

MRS. CONWAY (*to* KAY). Finish your charade now, dear.

(KAY *rises and goes up* C.)

ROBIN. Charade ! Can't I be in this ? I used to be an ace at charades.

MRS. CONWAY. No, dear, they're just finishing. We can have as many charades as we want now you're home for good. Have something to eat and talk to me while they're doing the last bit.

KAY (*up* C.). Come on, you two.

(HAZEL *moves up to* R. *of her and* CAROL *to* L. *of her.*)

We can collect Madge out there. Remember, it's an American party, and we can't have anything to drink, and then after kicking up a row, you ask who's giving the party, and then I'll say *Pussyfoot*——

(*She is going off with the others as she is saying this. Voices finish with door-slam.* ROBIN *settles down to the tray, which is on his knees. The beer bottle is on the floor.* MRS. CONWAY *watches him eat and drink with maternal delight. Both are happy and relaxed, at ease with each other.*)

MRS. CONWAY. Is there everything you want there, Robin ?

ROBIN (*with his mouth full*). Yes, thanks, Mother. Gosh, you don't know what it feels like to be out at last !

MRS. CONWAY. I do, you silly boy. What do you think I feel, to have you back at last—for good ?

ROBIN. I must get some clothes.

MRS. CONWAY. Yes, some really nice ones. Though it's a pity you can't keep on wearing that uniform. You look so smart in it. Poor Alan—he was only a corporal or something, y'know, and had the most hideous uniform, nothing seemed to fit him —Alan never looked *right* in the Army——

ROBIN. He's got a piffling sort of job at the Town Hall, hasn't he ?

MRS. CONWAY. Yes. He seems to like it, though. And perhaps he'll find something better later on.

ROBIN (*eagerly*). I've got all sorts of plans, y'know, Mother.

We've all been talking things over, in the mess. One of our chaps knows Jimmy White—you know, *the* Jimmy White— you've heard of him—and he thinks he can wangle me an intro- duction to him. My idea is something in the car and motor- bike line. I understand 'em, and I've heard people are buying like mad. And I have my gratuity, you know.

Mʀs. Cᴏɴᴡᴀʏ. Yes, dear, we'll have to talk about all that. There's plenty of time now, thank goodness! Don't you think all the girls are looking well?

Rᴏʙɪɴ (*eating and drinking away*). Yes, first rate, especially Hazel.

Mʀs. Cᴏɴᴡᴀʏ. Oh—of course Hazel's the one everybody notices. You ought to have seen the young men. And Kay— twenty-one—I can hardly believe it—but she's *very* grown-up and serious now—I don't know whether she'll make anything out of this writing of hers—but she is trying very hard—don't tease her too much, dear, she doesn't like it——

Rᴏʙɪɴ. I haven't been teasing her.

Mʀs. Cᴏɴᴡᴀʏ. No, but Hazel does sometimes—and I know what you children are. Madge has been teaching, you know, but she's trying for a much better school——

Rᴏʙɪɴ (*indifferently*). Good old Madge. I think I ought to go up to town for my clothes, Mother. You can't get anything really decent in Newlingham, and if I'm going to start selling cars I've got to look like somebody who knows a good suit when he sees one. (*There is a pause as he takes a long drink.*) Lord!—it's grand to be back again, and not just on a filthy little leave! (*He breaks off, as he looks at her, sitting quite close to him.*) Here, Mother—steady! (*He puts the tray on the floor* ʟ. *of him and puts his arms round her.*) Nothing to cry about now.

Mʀs. Cᴏɴᴡᴀʏ (*through her tears, smiling*). I know. That's why. You see, Robin—losing your father, then the War coming —taking you—I'm not used to happiness. I've forgotten about it. It's upsetting! And, Robin, now you are back— don't go rushing off again, *please*! Don't leave us—not for years and years. Let's all be cosy together and happy again, shall we?

(Jᴏᴀɴ *enters to above the ottoman, then stands awkwardly as she sees them together.* Mʀs. Cᴏɴᴡᴀʏ *turns and sees her. So does* Rᴏʙɪɴ, *and his face lights up.* Mʀs. Cᴏɴᴡᴀʏ *sees* Rᴏʙɪɴ's *face, then looks again at* Jᴏᴀɴ. *This should be played for as long as it will stand.*)

Jᴏᴀɴ (*rather nervously*). Oh—Mrs. Conway—they've finished the charade—and some people are going—and Madge asked me to tell you they're expecting you to sing something.

Mʀs. Cᴏɴᴡᴀʏ. Why didn't she come herself?

Jᴏᴀɴ (*rather faltering*). She and Kay and Carol began handing people sandwiches and things as soon as they finished **the** charade.

ROBIN (*rising and going to* L. *of* JOAN). Hello, Joan!

JOAN (*coming forward, thrilled*). Hello, Robin! Is it—nice to be back again?

ROBIN (*smiling, rather significantly*). Yes, of course.

MRS. CONWAY (*rising and speaking rather irritably*). Really, this room's a dreadful mess. (*Crossing below the ottoman to* R. *of it.*) I knew it would be. Hazel and Carol brought all these things down here. Joan, go and tell them they must take these things upstairs at once. I can't have this room looking like an old clothes' place. Perhaps you'd like to help them, dear.

JOAN. Yes—rather.

(*She smiles at* ROBIN *and goes.* MRS. CONWAY *takes* KAY'S *scarf from the desk down* R. *and puts it on the table up* R., *then crosses below* ROBIN *to pick up the tray from the floor below* L. *end of the chesterfield.*)

ROBIN (*crossing* L.). Here, let me, Mother! (*He picks up the tray for her, then faces her,* R. *of her.*) You're looking very artful, Mother.

MRS. CONWAY. Am I? I'm not feeling very artful. (*Carefully.*) Joan's grown up to be a very nice-looking girl, hasn't she?

ROBIN (*smiling*). Quite. (*He turns away and puts the tray on the table up* R.)

MRS. CONWAY (*in the same careful tone*). And I think she's got a pleasant easy disposition. Not very clever or go-ahead or anything like that. But a thoroughly *nice* girl.

ROBIN (*not eagerly*). Yes, I'll bet she is.

(*Voices off—*" Do ask her to sing," *etc.* HAZEL *sails in, to above the ottoman, to begin packing up the things. This should be done as quickly as possible.*)

HAZEL. They're all panting for a song, Mother. They don't even mind if it's German.

(ROBIN *goes to the desk down* R., *lights a cigarette and sits on the stool.*)

MRS. CONWAY. Thank goodness I was never so stupid as to stop singing German songs. What have Schubert and Schumann to do with Hindenburg and the Kaiser?

(CAROL *comes in, followed by* JOAN. CAROL *comes to* R. *of* MRS. CONWAY. JOAN *to the table up* R. HAZEL *goes with her armful.*)

CAROL (*loudly and cheerfully*). Everybody guessed the charade, just because it was Pussyfoot—

(**MRS. CONWAY** *caresses her.*)

—though they hadn't guessed *any* of the syllables. All except Mr. James, who thought it was *kinema* (*hard* " *k* "). (*She goes to the chair* L. *of the table up* R. *for a bundle of clothes.*) When they say "Kinema" I can't believe I've ever been to one. It sounds like some other kind of place.

(MRS. CONWAY *puts box of hats and moustaches on top of her bundle.*)

Robin, have you seen William S. Hart ?
    ROBIN. Yes.
    CAROL (*pausing with her armful, very solemnly*). I *love* William S. Hart. I wonder what " S " stands for ?
    ROBIN. Sidney.
    CAROL (*in horror*). Robin, it *doesn't* !

(*She goes out.* JOAN *now has the remainder of the things, all of which should now be cleared, except for a few pieces on the ottoman.*)

    MRS. CONWAY. Come along, Robin, I may want you and Alan to move the piano for me. Bring the tray, dear.

(MRS. CONWAY *goes out.*)

ROBIN. Righto.

(*He picks up the tray from the table up* R., *and with a smile at* JOAN *goes off.* JOAN *follows with a bundle of clothes. They have all gone out. Sounds of the party now, voices, laughs, clinks of glasses,* ROBIN'S *voice, etc. This is not a mere " wait," but deliberate atmosphere. Then* KAY *enters quickly and eagerly, and finds a pad of paper and pencil in the drawer of the desk down* R. *She frowns and thinks, then makes some rapid notes, sitting on the* R. *arm of the chesterfield, facing* C. *Door-slam and voices stop as* CAROL *looks in and comes to above the ottoman to collect the few remaining clothes.*)

    CAROL (*with awe, very charming*). Kay, have you suddenly been *inspired* ? (*She has come to* R. *of* KAY.)
    KAY (*looking up, very serious*). No, not really. But I'm bursting with all kinds of feelings and thoughts and impressions —you know——
    CAROL. Oh yes—so am I. Millions and millions. I couldn't possibly *begin* to write them.
    KAY. No, but in my novel, a girl goes to a party—you see —and there are some things I've been feeling—very subtle things—that I *know* she'd feel—and I want my novel to be very real this time—so I had to scribble them down——
    CAROL. Will you tell me them afterwards ?
    KAY. Yes.
    CAROL. Bedroom ?
    KAY. Yes, if you're not too sleepy.

CAROL (*solemnly*). I couldn't be. Kay, I think you're *won derful.*

(MRS. CONWAY *is heard off singing*—" *Der Nussbaum,*" *quietly at first and swelling when* CAROL *says* " Both of you are " *until fall of* CURTAIN.)

KAY (*solemnly*). I think *life's* wonderful.
CAROL (*quite solemnly*). Both of you are.

CAROL *withdraws.* KAY *writes for another moment, then, moved by what she has written, puts down paper and pencil. There is about her that sense of the sudden ecstasy of creation.*

The accompaniment of MRS. CONWAY'S *song is now heard.* KAY, *moving towards the exit, is arrested by this. She quietly switches off the lights inside the room. She draws open the curtains at the window and sits down on the window-seat, looking off* L., *listening in a sort of ecstatic reverie, quite still. As* KAY *listens, without moving a finger, staring away from the exit, not* **at** *something but* into *something, and the song goes* **on,**

The CURTAIN *slowly and quietly descends.*

ACT II

SCENE.—*The same. The present time.*
*At first sight it would appear that the room is not much altered,
but then we see that a great deal must have happened. There is
a different wallpaper, the furniture has been changed, the pictures
and books are not altogether the same as before, and we notice
a wireless set. The general effect should be shabbier than before,
though the room appears harder and rather brighter than it was
during the party in 1919.*
(See Photograph of Scene.)

At the rise of the CURTAIN, *KAY is discovered in exactly the same
place and posture she was in at the end of Act I—sitting on the
window-seat looking out towards L. Sh* is fairly smartly dressed,
*in town clothes, efficiently rather than decoratively. She has not
changed a great deal, but is thinner, finer-drawn, much harder.
She seems lost in a not very pleasant reverie. After a few mo-
ments,* ALAN *enters. He has aged a good deal, is grey, and is
comfortably shabby. He is as shy and awkward as ever, but
there is about him a certain quiet inner poise, an inward certainty
and serenity, missing from all the others.*

ALAN (*below the desk up* R.—*quietly*). Well—Kay.
KAY (*happily*). Alan!

*(She jumps up and kisses him. Then they look at each other,
smiling a little. He rubs his hands in embarrassment, as he
always did.)*

ALAN. I'm glad you could come. It was the only thing about
this business that didn't make me hate the thought of it—the
chance *you* might be able to come. But Mother says you're not
staying the night.
KAY. I can't, Alan. I must get back to London to-night.
(She closes the curtains at the window.)
ALAN. Work?
KAY (*moving to the chair* L. *of the table* C. *and sitting*). Yes. I
have to go to Southampton in the morning—to write a nice little
piece about the newest little film star.
ALAN. Do you often have to do that?
KAY. Yes, Alan, quite often. There are an awful lot of
film stars and they're always arriving at Southampton, except

33

when they arrive at Plymouth—damn their eyes ! And all
the women readers of the " *Daily Courier* " like to read a bright
half-column about their glamorous favourites.

ALAN (*above the table* c.—*thoughtfully*). They look very nice
—but all rather alike.

KAY (*decidedly*). They *are* all rather alike—and so are my
bright interviews with 'em. In fact, sometimes I feel we're
all just going round and round, like poor old circus ponies.

ALAN (*after a pause*). Are you writing another novel ?

KAY (*very quietly*). No, my dear, I'm not. (*She pauses,
then gives a short laugh.*) I tell myself too many people are
writing novels.

ALAN. Well, it does look like that—sometimes.

KAY. Yes. But that's not the real reason. I still feel
mine wouldn't be like theirs—anyhow, not the next, even if
the last was. But—as things are—I just can't . . .

(ALAN *moves to the fireplace* L.)

ALAN (*after a pause*). The last time you wrote, Kay—I mean
to me—you sounded rather unhappy, I thought.

KAY (*with self-reproach*). I was. I suppose that's why I
suddenly remembered you—and wrote. Not very flattering—
to you—is it ?

ALAN (*with cheerful modesty*). In a way it is, y'know. Yes,
Kay, I'd take that as a compliment.

KAY (*with sudden burst of affection*). Alan ! And I loathe
that coat you're wearing. It doesn't match the rest of you,
does it ?

ALAN (*stammering, apologetic*). No—well, you see—I just
wear it in the house—an old coat—just as a house coat—it
saves my other one—I oughtn't to have put it on to-night.
Just habit, y'know. I'll change it before the others come . . .
Why were you so unhappy then—the last time you wrote ?

KAY (*after a short pause*). Something—that was always
ending—really did come to an end just then. It had lasted
ten years—off and on—and eating more of one's life away when
it was off than when it was on. He was married. There were
children. It was the usual nasty muddle—— (*She breaks off.*)
Alan, you don't know what day it is to-day.

ALAN (*chuckling*). But I do, I do. And of course Mother
did too. Look ! (*He pulls a small package out of his pocket
and holds it out to her.*)

KAY (*after jumping up, taking it and kissing him*). Alan, you're
an angel ! I never thought I'd have another single birthday
present. And you know how old I am now ? Forty. *Forty !*

ALAN (*smiling*). I'm forty-four. And it's all right, y'know.
You'll like it.

(*The front-door bell rings.*)

Look at your present. I hope it's all right. (*He crosses above the table* c. *to the front door.*)
JOAN (*off*). Hullo, Alan.

(KAY *hastily unwraps her parcel and takes out a hideous, cheap little handbag. She looks at it and does not know whether to laugh or cry over the thing. Meanwhile* ALAN *has brought in* JOAN, *now* JOAN CONWAY, *for she married* ROBIN. *Time has not been very kind to her. She is now a rather sloppy, querulous woman of forty-one. Her voice has a very irritating quality.* KAY *comes below the table to meet* JOAN *and kisses her.* ALAN *sits on the upstage arm of the chesterfield down* R.)

(*Who runs on querulously.*) Hello, Kay. I didn't think you'd manage to be here—you hardly ever do come to Newlingham now, do you ? And I must say I don't blame you—— (*She breaks off because she notices the awful handbag.*) Oh—what a——
KAY (L. *of the table* c.—*forcefully*). Nice, isn't it ? Alan has just given it to me. How are the children ?
JOAN (*sitting* R. *of the table* c., *putting her bag on the table and taking off her gloves*). Richard's very well, but the doctor says Ann's tonsils ought to come out—though he doesn't tell me who's to pay for the operation, never thinks about that. They did enjoy those things you sent at Christmas, Kay—I don't know what they'd have done without them, though I did my best.
KAY. I'm sure you did, Joan.
JOAN. Alan was very good to them too, weren't you, Alan ? Though of course it's not like their having a father ——(*She breaks off and looks miserably at* KAY.) You know, I haven't seen Robin for months. Some people say I ought to divorce him, but—I don't know—— (*With sudden misery.*) Honestly, isn't it awful ? Oh—Kay—— (*She suddenly giggles.*) Doesn't that sound silly— Oh—Kay——
KAY (*wearily, moving to the fireplace* L.). No, I've stopped noticing it.
JOAN. Richard's always saying okay—he's heard it at the pictures—and of course Ann copies him—— (*She breaks off and looks anxiously at them both.*) Do you think it's all right, my coming here to-night ? It was Hazel who told me you were having a sort of family meeting, and she thought I ought to be here, and I think so too. But Granny Conway didn't ask me——
KAY. (*with a sudden laugh*). Joan, you don't call Mother Granny Conway ?
JOAN. Well, I got into the habit, y'know, with the children——
KAY. She must loathe it.
ALAN (*apologetically, to* JOAN). I think she does, you know.
JOAN. I must try and remember. Is she upstairs ?

ALAN. Yes. Madge is here too.

(JOAN *rises and picks up her bag and gloves from the table.*)

JOAN (*nerving herself*). I think—I'll go up and ask her if it's
all right—my staying—otherwise I'd feel such a fool.

(*She goes to the arch.* ALAN *rises.*)

KAY. Yes, do. And tell her we think you ought to be here
—if you *want* to be——

JOAN (*coming back a little* R.C.). Well, it isn't that—but—
you see—if it's about money—I must know something, mustn't
I ? After all, I'm Robin's wife—and Richard and Ann are his
children——

ALAN (*kindly, above the chesterfield* R.). Yes, Joan, you tell
Mother that, if she objects. But she won't, though.

(JOAN *looks at them a moment, doubtful, then goes. They watch
her go, then look at one another.* KAY *picks up her birthday
present from the table* C. *and takes it to the desk up* R.)

KAY (*lowering her voice a little*). I suppose Robin's pretty
hopeless—but really, Joan's such a fool——

ALAN (*with a slow shrewdness*). Yes, but the way Robin's
treated her has made her feel more of a fool than she really is.
It's taken away all her confidence in herself, you see, Kay.
Otherwise, she mightn't have been so bad.

KAY (*coming down to sit on the chair* R. *of the table*). You used
to like Joan, didn't you ?

ALAN (*looking at her, then slowly smiling*). You remember
when she and Robin told us they were engaged ? I was in
love with her then. It was the only time I ever fell in love
with anybody. (*Crossing to above the table* C.) And I remember
—quite suddenly hating Robin—yes, really hating him. None
of this loving and hating lasted, of course—it was just silly stuff.
But I remember it quite well.

KAY. Suppose it had been you instead of Robin——

ALAN (*hastily, crossing to the fireplace* L.). Oh—no, that
wouldn't have done at all. Really it wouldn't. Most unsuitable !

(KAY *laughs in affectionate amusement at his bachelor's horror.*
MADGE *enters. She is very different from the girl of Act I.
She has short greyish hair, wears glasses, and is neatly but severely
dressed. She speaks with a dry precision, but underneath her
assured schoolmistress manner is a suggestion of the neurotic
woman. She carries a copy of " Time and Tide." She goes
to the desk up* R. *and opens three drawers, looking for an envelope.*)

MADGE (*very decisively*). I've just told Mother that if I hadn't
happened to be in the neighbourhood to-day—I've applied for a
headship at Borderton, you know, Kay, and had my interview

there this afternoon—nothing would have induced me to be here to-night.

KAY. Well, I don't know why you bothered telling her, Madge. You *are* here, that's all that matters.

MADGE. No, it isn't. (*She comes down* R. *of the table* C. *to look in the downstage drawer.*) I want her to understand quite clearly that I've no further interest in these family muddles, financial or otherwise. (*She goes up* L. *of the table* C., *moves the chair and finds an envelope in the* L. *drawer of the table.*) Also that I would have thought it unnecessary to ask for a day away from my work at Collingfield in order to attend one of these ridiculous hysterical conferences.

KAY. You talk as if you'd been dragged here every few weeks.

MADGE. No, I haven't. But I've had a great many more of these silly discussions than you have—please remember, Kay. Mother and Gerald Thornton seem to imagine that the time of a woman journalist in London is far more precious than that of a senior mistress at a large girls' public school. Why—I can't think. But the result is, I've been dragged in often when you haven't. (*She goes up to the desk up* R. *for an ink-bottle to fill her fountain-pen.*)

KAY (*rather wearily*). All right. But seeing we're both here now, let's make the best of it.

ALAN (*eagerly, hopefully*). Yes, of course.

MADGE (*coming back to above the table* C. *and filling her pen—distastefully*). Joan's here. I hope there's no chance of Robin coming too. That's something you've missed so far, I think, Kay. I've had one experience of their suddenly meeting here —Robin half-drunk, ready to insult everybody, Joan weeping and resentful—the pair of them discussing every unpleasant detail of their private life—and it's not an experience I want to repeat.

KAY (*half serious, half lightly*). I don't blame you, Madge. But for the Lord's sake, be human to-night. You're not talking to the Collingfield common room now. This is your nice brother Alan. I'm your nice sister Kay. We know all about you——

MADGE (*sitting* L. *of the table to address her envelope*). That's just where you're wrong. You know hardly anything about me, any of you. The life you don't see—call it the Collingfield common room if that amuses you—is my real life. It represents exactly the sort of person I am now, and what you and Alan and Mother remember—and trust Mother not to forget anything foolish and embarrassing—is no longer of any importance at all.

KAY (*rather earnestly*). I'd hate to think that, Madge.

ALAN (*shyly, earnestly*). And it isn't true. It really isn't. Because—— (*He hesitates, and is lost.*)

MADGE (*not too unkindly*). I heard your extraordinary views the last time I was here, Alan. I also discussed them with

Herrickson—our senior maths. mistress and a most brilliant woman—and she demolished them very thoroughly.

KAY (*more to cheer him up*). You tell me, Alan, if there's time later on. We're not going to be trampled on by any of Madge's Miss What's-her-names. And we don't care how brilliant they are, do we, Alan ?

(ALAN *grins and rubs his hands.* MADGE *deliberately changes the subject.*)

MADGE (*taking the ink-bottle back to the desk up* R., *then crossing to the small table up* L. *to take a cigarette*). Are you doing anything besides this popular journalism now, Kay ? Have you begun another book ?

KAY (*rather shortly*). No.

MADGE. Pity, isn't it ?

KAY (*after a pause, looking steadily at her*). What about you, Madge ? Are you building Jerusalem—in England's green and pleasant land ?

MADGE (*abruptly*). Possibly not. (*She lights her cigarette and returns to above the table* C.) But I'm trying to put a little knowledge of history and a little sense into the heads of a hundred and fifty middle-class girls. It's hard work and useful work. Certainly nothing to be ashamed of.

KAY (*looking hard and speaking very quietly*). Then—why be ashamed ?

MADGE (*instantly, loudly*). I'm not. (*She turns up to the window.*)

(HAZEL *enters from outside. She is extremely well-dressed, the best dressed of them all, and has not lost her looks, but there is something noticeably subdued, fearful, about her. She comes* R.C. KAY *rises to* L. *of her and they kiss.*)

HAZEL. Hullo, Madge—Kay !

KAY. Hazel, my dear, you're grander every time I see you.

HAZEL (*glancing in the mirror above the chesterfield down* R.). Do you like it ?

KAY. Yes—and you didn't get that in Newlingham—at the Bon Marché ! Do you remember when we used to think the Bon Marché marvellous ?

HAZEL (*brightening up at this*). Yes—and now they seem ghastly. Well, that's something, isn't it ? (*She realizes that this gives her away, so hastily asks.*) Is Joan here ? (*She crosses below the table to* ALAN *at the fireplace* L.)

ALAN. Yes. She's upstairs with Mother. Is Ernest coming to-night ?

(KAY *sits on the chesterfield* R., *and picks up a book which is lying there.*)

HAZEL (*hesitating*). I—don't—know.

MADGE (*above the table* C.—*coldly*). I thought it was understood he was coming. Mother thinks he is. I believe she's rather counting on him.

HAZEL (*hastily*). Well, she mustn't. (*She sits in the arm-chair* L.) I've told her not to. I don't even know yet if he'll be here at all.

(ALAN *sits in the chair below the fire.*)

MADGE (*annoyed*). But this is ridiculous. We're told that things are desperate. Kay and I have to leave our work, travel miles and miles, stop thinking about anything else, and now you don't even know if your own husband will walk down the road to be here.

HAZEL. But you know what Ernest is ? He said he *might* come to-night. I asked him again only at lunch-time to-day —and he said he didn't know—and then I didn't like——

MADGE (*cutting in sharply*). Didn't like ! You mean you *daren't*. That miserable little——

HAZEL (*protesting*). Madge ! Please stop.

(MADGE *looks at her in contempt, picks up her things from the table, then walks off.* HAZEL *looks very miserable.*)

KAY (*rising with her book and sitting* R. *of the table* O.). How are the children ?

HAZEL. Peter has a cold again—poor lamb—he's always getting colds. Margaret's all right. Never *any* trouble with her. She's been doing some ballet dancing, y'know, and the teacher thinks she's *marvellous* for her age. Oh—you forgot her last birthday, Kay. The child was *so* disappointed.

KAY. I'm sorry. Tell her I'll make up for it at Christmas. I must have been away on a job or something——

HAZEL (*eagerly*). I read your article on Glyrna Foss—you know, about three months ago—when she came over from Hollywood. Did she really say all those things to you, Kay, or did you make them up ?

KAY (*with a sort of quiet weariness*). She said some of them. The rest I made up.

HAZEL (*eagerly*). Did she say anything about Leo Frobisher —her husband, y'know, and they'd just separated ?

KAY. Yes, but I didn't print it.

HAZEL (*all eagerness*). What did she say ?

KAY. She said—(*imitating a very bad type of American voice*) " I'll bet that God-forgotten left-over ham husband of mine gets himself poured out o' the next boat." (*In a normal voice, dryly.*) You'd like her, Hazel. She's a sweet child.

HAZEL. She sounds awful, but I suppose you can't judge by the way they talk, using all that slang. And I know you don't think you're very lucky, Kay——

KAY. I vary. Sometimes when I manage to remember what

most women go through, all kinds of women all over the world, I don't think, I *know* I'm lucky. But usually—I feel clean out of luck.

HAZEL. I know, that's what I say. But I think you're *very* lucky, meeting all these people, and being in London and all that. Look at me, still in Newlingham, and I *loathe* Newlingham, and it gets worse and worse. Doesn't it, Alan—though I don't suppose you notice ?

ALAN (*mildly*). I think it's about the same—perhaps we get worse, that's all.

HAZEL (*looking at him in a sort of impersonal fashion*). Somebody was saying to me only the other day how queer they thought you were, Alan, And you are—really, aren't you ? I mean you don't seem to bother about everything as most people do. I've often wondered whether you're happy inside or just dull. But I often wonder about people like that—(*to* KAY) don't you ? Though I suppose being so clever now, and a writer and everything, you *know* about them. But I don't. And I simply can't tell from what people look like. We had a maid, y'know, Jessie, and she seemed such a cheerful little thing —always smiling and humming—Ernest used to get quite cross with her—she was *too* cheerful really—and then suddenly she took over twenty aspirins all at once, we had to have the doctor and everything, and she said it was simply because she couldn't bear it any longer—she'd had enough of *everything*, she said. Isn't it strange ?

KAY. But you must feel like that sometimes, don't you ?

HAZEL. Yes, I do. But I'm always surprised when other people do, because somehow they never *look* it. Oh—— (*She stops short, rises and goes to* L. *of the table* O., *then lowers her voice.*) Robin rang me up yesterday—he's living in Leicester just now, you know—and I told him about to-night—and he said he might look in because he wouldn't be far away.

ALAN. I hope he doesn't.

KAY. What's he doing now, Hazel ?

HAZEL. I don't know really—he's always changing, y'know —but it's something to do with commission.

MRS. CONWAY (*off*). Hang your coat there, Joan.

HAZEL. Shall I tell Joan he might be coming here ?

KAY. No. Risk it.

(KAY *doesn't say any more because* MRS. CONWAY *comes in, followed by* JOAN. MRS. CONWAY *is now a woman of sixty-five and not a very well-preserved specimen. She has not gone neat and modern, but kept to her full-blown Edwardian type, so that now she looks an impressive but unpleasant ruin, decked out in shabby finery. There is just a suggestion in her manner that she might be drinking rather more than is good for her. She comes* R.O. ; JOAN *to the desk up* R.)

MRS. CONWAY. Now then, Hazel, haven't you brought Ernest with you ?

HAZEL (*rather timidly*). No, Mother. I hope—he'll be here soon.

MRS. CONWAY. Of course he will. Well, we can't do anything until Gerald arrives. He knows how things are—exactly. Where's Madge ?

KAY. I thought she went upstairs.

MRS. CONWAY. She's probably taking something in the bathroom. (*She crosses below the table to the switch above the fireplace to turn on the brackets.*) I've never known anybody who took so many things as poor Madge. She's given herself so many lotions and gargles and sprays that no man has ever looked twice at her—poor thing. (*By the fireplace.*) Alan, I think we ought to have both port and whisky out, don't you ? I told the girl to leave it all ready in the dining-room. Better bring it in.

(ALAN *rises and goes out, crossing below the table.*)

(*Crossing in front of* HAZEL *to* C., *above the table.*) Now what I'm wondering is this—should we all sit round looking very stiff and formal—y'know, make it a proper business affair, because after all, it *is* a business affair—or should we make everybody comfortable and *cosy* ? (*She passes on in front of* JOAN *to up* R.) What do you think ?

KAY. I think—Mother—you're enjoying this.

(HAZEL *and* JOAN *move* L. *after* MRS. CONWAY *passes them.* HAZEL *sits in the chair below the fire ;* JOAN *sits on the pouffe.*)

MRS. CONWAY. Well, after all, why shouldn't I ? It's nice to see all you children at home again. Even Madge.

(MADGE *enters.* MRS. CONWAY *probably saw her before, but undoubtedly sees her now.*)

I say it's nice to see all you children home again—even you, Madge.

MADGE (R.C.). I'm not a child and this is no longer my home.

MRS. CONWAY (*sharply, slightly above* L. *of* MADGE). You were a child once—and a very troublesome one, too—and for twenty years this was your home—and please don't talk in that tone to me. You're not in a classroom now, remember.

(MADGE *goes to the chesterfield down* R.)

HAZEL. Now—Mother—please—it's not going to be easy to-night—and——

MADGE (*coldly*). Don't worry, Hazel. Mother enjoys things not being easy.

(*She sits down on the chesterfield* R., *and may be doing the crossword puzzle in her " Time and Tide " during the next scene.* MRS. CONWAY *observes her maliciously, then turns to* KAY.)

MRS. CONWAY. Kay, *who* was the man the Philipsons saw you dining with at the—what's the name of that restaurant ?

(MRS. CONWAY *has started to drag the chair* L. *of the desk to above the table* C. KAY *rises and takes the* R. *arm of it to help her.*)

KAY. The Ivy, Mother. And the man is a man called Hugo Steel. (*She sits* R. *of the table again.*) I've told you already.

MRS. CONWAY (*smoothly*). Yes, dear, but you didn't tell me much. The Philipsons said you seemed awfully friendly together. I suppose he's an old friend ?

KAY (*shortly*). Yes.

(MRS. CONWAY *has placed the chair above the table and now comes down* R. *of the table to behind* KAY *and leans over her.*)

MRS. CONWAY. Isn't it a pity—you couldn't—I mean, if he's a really nice man.

KAY (*trying to cut it short*). Yes, a great pity.

MRS. CONWAY. I've so often hoped you'd be settled with some nice man—and when the Philipsons told me——

KAY (*rather harshly*). Mother, I'm forty to-day. Had you forgotten ?

MRS. CONWAY. Of course I hadn't. (*Going round above the table to* L. *of it.*) A mother *always* remembers. Joan——

JOAN (*whose attention has been elsewhere, turning*). Yes, Grannie Conway ?

MRS. CONWAY (*crossly*). Don't call me that ridiculous name.

JOAN. I forgot, I'm sorry.

MRS. CONWAY. Didn't I tell you it was Kay's birthday ? I've something for you, too—— (*She goes to her bag which she has put down on the* L. *side of the table to get a small jewel-case from it.*)

KAY (*rising*). No, Mother, you mustn't—really——

MRS. CONWAY (*producing a small diamond brooch*). There ! (*She moves to below the table* C.) Your father gave me that, the second Christmas after we were married, and it's a charming little brooch. Brazilian diamonds. It was an old piece then. Look at the colour in the stones. You always get that in the old South American diamonds. There now !

KAY (*gently*). It's very sweet of you, Mother, but really I'd rather not take this from you.

MRS. CONWAY. Don't be absurd. It's mine, and now I give it to you. (*She takes her hand and puts the brooch in it.*) Take it or I'll be cross. And many happy returns, of course.

(KAY *takes the brooch, then, suddenly rather moved, kisses her mother. She then goes to the desk up* R. ALAN *enters with a tray with port, whisky, soda and glasses and puts it on the small table up* L.)

When you were younger, I never liked you as much as I did Hazel, but now I think I was wrong.

HAZEL. Oh—Mother !

MRS. CONWAY. I know, Hazel dear, but you're such a *fool* with that little husband of yours. Why, if he were mine——

HAZEL (*sharply for her*). Well, he isn't—and you really know very little about him.

MRS. CONWAY (*going below the table and up* R. *of it*). It's time the men were here. I've always hated seeing a lot of women sitting about, with no men. (*She pauses on her way to say this at* MADGE.) *They* always look silly, and then I feel silly myself. I don't know why. (*Now arrived above the table, she notices* ALAN. *With some malice.*) Of course you're here, Alan. I was forgetting you. Or forgetting you were a man.

ALAN (*mildly, by the small table up* L.). I must grow a shaggy beard and drum on my chest and ro-o-ar !

JOAN (*brightly*). When their Uncle Frank—you know, Freda's husband, they live in London—took the children to the Zoo for the first time, little Richard was only five—and there was an enormous monkey—what Alan said reminded me of it—and——

MRS. CONWAY (*cutting this ruthlessly*). Would anybody like a glass of port ? (*She crosses to the small table up* L. ALAN *makes way by passing below her and up to the window-seat.*) Kay ? Hazel ? What about you, Madge ? It's a scholarly wine. You remember what Meredith wrote about it in " The Egoist." But nobody reads Meredith now and nobody takes port. I used to read Meredith when I was a girl and thought I was very clever. But I didn't like port then. Now I don't care about Meredith. (*She has poured herself out a glass of port and, crossing to above the table, begins drinking it quickly.*) It's not good port this— even I know that, though men always say women don't know anything about it—but it's rich and warming, even this—like a handsome compliment. That's gone too. Nobody pays compliments any more—except old Doctor Halliday, who's well over eighty and has no memory at all. He talked to me for half an hour the other day, thinking I was Mrs. Rushbury——

(*There is a ring at the bell.* ALAN *goes off.*)

There ! That's probably Gerald.

MADGE (*wearily*). At last !

MRS. CONWAY (*maliciously*). Yes, Madge, but you mustn't be so impatient.

(MADGE *glares at her.* Voices off," Hullo, Alan," " Hullo, Gerald," *etc. Enter* GERALD, *carrying a brief-case. He is over fifty now, and though careful of his appearance, he looks it. He is grey and wears glasses. He is much drier and harder than he was in Act I. Until* GERALD *opens the meeting, there should be the appearance of general dialogue, as a background to the actual dialogue as follows.*)

(*Shaking hands with him below the table.*) Well, Gerald, will you have a drink before you begin talking ?

GERALD. No, thank you. (*He smiles quickly, falsely, then turns away.*)

(MRS. CONWAY *looks at him sharply, then goes to the table up* L. GERALD *turns to* KAY.)

How are you, Kay ?

KAY (*coming down to* L. *of* GERALD *down* R.C.). Quite well, thank you, Gerald. (*She stares at him.*) I'm sorry, but it's true.

GERALD. What is ?

KAY. I always remember your saying, years ago, that you didn't mind living in Newlingham, but you were determined to be as different as possible from the Newlingham type of man.

GERALD (*hastily, frowning a little*). I don't remember saying that——

KAY. Yes, you did. And now—I'm sorry, Gerald, but it's true—you suddenly look like *all* those Newlingham men rolled into one——

GERALD (*rather shortly*). What do I do ? Apologize ?

(*He turns away, leaving her regarding him speculatively, then crosses below the table to* L. *to shake hands with* HAZEL. *Enter* ALAN, *followed by* ERNEST, *who looks far more prosperous than he did before and has lost his early shyness. He is nearly fifty now and, if anything, looks older.* ALAN *goes to the window-seat.* ERNEST *comes to* R.C.)

ERNEST. Good evening, Kay.

(*He shakes hands with her. She goes up to the window-seat.*)

MRS. CONWAY (L. *of the table* C.). Good evening, Ernest.

ERNEST. Good evening.

(MRS. CONWAY *extends a hand to him across the table, but he only flicks the ash off his cigar into the ashtray on the table.*)

HAZEL (*who has crossed to below the table* C.). Oh—Ernest— I'm so glad you're here——

ERNEST (R. *of the table* C., *with a cold contempt*). You are, eh ?

HAZEL (*her face falling, resentfully*). I suppose that means you won't stay now—just to show me——

ERNEST. I don't need to show you. You know, by this time.

HAZEL (*lowering her voice*). Ernest—please—be nice to them to-night—especially to Mother—you could be such a help if you wanted to be——

ERNEST (*cutting through this*). I don't know what you're talking about.

(*They both notice then that* MADGE *is quite near, regarding them with a contemptuous smile.* ERNEST *gives her a sharp look, then turns away to the desk up* R. HAZEL *looks deeply embarrassed, then looks as if she was about to appeal to* MADGE.)

MADGE (*on the chesterfield* R.—*coolly*). I shouldn't say a word, if I were you, Hazel. I mean to me. It would only make it worse.

MRS. CONWAY (*in a loud cheerful tone, clapping her hands*). Now then, everybody, please be quiet and pay attention. Now then, Hazel, stop fidgeting there and sit down.

(HAZEL *crosses and sits in the chair below the fire.* KAY *sits* R. *of the table.* GERALD *sits above the table.* MRS. CONWAY *sits* L. *of the table.* ERNEST *sits on the edge of the desk up* R. ALAN *remains standing up* L.C., *slightly* L. *of the window.* JOAN *is still seated on the pouffe.*)

We must be very business-like, mustn't we, Gerald ? I'm so glad you were able to come, Ernest. You'll help us to be business-like, won't you ?

ERNEST (*grimly*). Yes.

MADGE. And that doesn't mean you're at liberty to make yourself unpleasant.

MRS. CONWAY (*sharply*). Be quiet, Madge. (*Turning, with a smile and great social air, to* GERALD.) Now then, Gerald, we're all waiting. Tell us all about it.

(GERALD, *who has been glancing at his papers, looks up at her and round the waiting circle with a sort of despair, as if to ask what could be done with such people.*)

GERALD (*in a dry legal tone*). Acting under instructions from Mrs. Conway, after it was decided you should all meet here, I have prepared a short statement of Mrs. Conway's present financial position——

MRS. CONWAY (*protesting*). Gerald !

GERALD (*rather despairing*). Yes ?

MRS. CONWAY. Must you talk in that awful dry, inhuman way ? I mean, after all, I've known you since you were a boy, and the children have known you all their lives, and you're beginning to talk as if you'd never seen any of us before. And it sounds so horrid.

GERALD. But I'm not here now as a friend of the family, but as your solicitor.

MRS. CONWAY (*with dignity*). No. You're here as a friend of the family who also happens to be my solicitor. And I think it would be much better if you told us all in a simple, friendly way what the position is.

ALAN. I think that would be better, you know, Gerald.

KAY. So do I. When you turn on that legal manner, I can't

take you seriously—I feel you're still acting in one of our old charades.

HAZEL (*with sudden warmth*). Oh—weren't they fun ! And you were so good in them, Gerald. Why can't we have some more——

ERNEST (*brutally*). What—at your age ? (*He turns back to an evening paper he has been reading.*)

HAZEL. I don't see why not. Mother was older than we are now when she used to play——

GERALD (*rather cuttingly*). You're not proposing to turn this into a charade, are you, Hazel ?

KAY. What a pity it isn't one !

ALAN (*very quietly*). Perhaps it is.

MRS. CONWAY. Now don't *you* start being silly, Alan. Now then, Gerald, just tell us how things are—and don't read out a lot of figures and dates and things—I know you've brought them with you—but keep them for anybody who wants to have a look at them—perhaps *you'd* like to have a look at them afterwards, Ernest——

ERNEST. I might. (*To* GERALD.) Go ahead.

GERALD (*dryly*). Well, the position is this. Mrs. Conway for a long time now has derived her income from two sources. A holding in Farrow and Conway Limited. And some property in Newlingham, the houses at the north end of Church Road. Farrow and Conway were hit badly by the slump and have not recovered yet. The houses in Church Road are not worth anything like what they were, and the only chance of making that property pay is to convert the houses into flats. But this would demand a substantial outlay of capital. Mrs. Conway has received an offer for her holding in Farrow and Conway Limited. But it would not pay for the reconstruction of the Church Road property. Meanwhile that property may soon be a liability instead of an asset. So, you see, the position is very serious.

MADGE (*coldly*). I must say I'm very much surprised. I always understood that Mother was left extremely well provided for.

MRS. CONWAY (*proudly*). Certainly I was. Your father saw to that.

GERALD. Both the shares and the property have declined in value.

MADGE (*rising*). Yes, but even so—I'm still surprised. Mother must have been very extravagant.

GERALD. Mrs. Conway hasn't been as careful as she might have been.

MRS. CONWAY. There were six of you to bring up and educate——

MADGE (R. *of the table* o.). It isn't that. I know how much *we* cost. It's since then that the money's been spent. And I know who must have had most of it—Robin !

MRS. CONWAY (*angry now*). That'll do, Madge. It was my money——

MADGE. It wasn't. It was only yours to hold in trust for us. (*Moving to above the table* C.) Alan, you're the eldest and you've been here all the time, why didn't you do something ?

ALAN. I'm afraid—I—haven't bothered much about—these things——

MADGE (*with growing force*). Then you ought to have done. (*She moves down* L. *of* MRS. CONWAY.) I think it's absolutely wicked. I've been working hard earning my living for over twenty years, and I've looked forward to having something from what Father left, enough to pay for a few really good holidays or to buy myself a little house of my own—and now it's all gone—just because Mother and Robin between them have flung it away——

MRS. CONWAY (*angrily*). You ought to be ashamed of yourself, talking like that ! What if I have helped Robin ? He needed it, and I'm his mother. If you'd needed it, I'd have helped you too——

MADGE (L.C.). You wouldn't. When I told you I had a chance to buy a partnership in that school, you only laughed at me——

MRS. CONWAY. Because you were all right where you were and didn't need to buy any partnerships.

MADGE. And Robin did, I suppose ?

MRS. CONWAY. Yes, because he's a man—with a wife and children to support. This is just typical of you, Madge. Call yourself a Socialist and blame people for taking an interest in money, and then it turns out you're the most mercenary of us all.

MADGE. I don't call myself a Socialist—though that's nothing to do with it—— (*She sits in the armchair* L.)

ERNEST (*rising and breaking in brutally*). How long does this go on ? Because I've something else to do. (*He sits on the upstage arm of the chesterfield* R.)

MRS. CONWAY (*trying hard to placate him*). That's all right, Ernest. Look what you've done now, Madge. Made Joan cry.

JOAN (*suddenly weeping quietly in the background*). I'm sorry —I just—remembered—so many things—that's all.

GERALD. At the present moment, Mrs. Conway has a considerable overdraft at the bank. Now there are two possible courses of action. One is to sell the houses for what they'll fetch, and to hold on to the shares. But I warn you that the houses won't fetch much. The alternative is to sell the shares, then to raise an additional sum—probably between two or three thousand pounds—and to convert the houses into flats——

MRS. CONWAY (*hopefully*). We've had a sort of scheme from an architect, and really it looks most attractive. There'd be at least thirty nice flats, and you know what people will pay for flats nowadays. Don't you think it's a splendid idea, Ernest ?

(ERNEST *does not reply.* MRS. CONWAY *smiles at him and then her smile falters, but she returns hopefully to the theme.*)

I felt if we all discussed it in a nice friendly way, we could decide something. I know you business men like everything cut-and-dried, but I believe it's better to be nice and friendly. It isn't true that people will only do things for money. I'm always being surprised about that. People are *very* nice and kind, really—— (*She breaks off, looks at the women, then continues in a more intimate tone.*) Only last week I went to old Mrs. Jepson's funeral, and I was walking back through the cemetery with Mrs. Whitehead—I hadn't been round there for years—and I saw Carol's grave—and of course I was rather upset, suddenly coming on it like that—but it was so beautifully kept, with flowers—lovely flowers—growing there. And I thought, now there's an instance—nobody's told them to do that or paid them for it—it's just natural kindness——

MADGE (*harshly*). No it isn't. Somebody must have been paying for it.

KAY (*turning*). Alan ! It must be you. Isn't it ?

ALAN. Well—I do send them something—once ^very year, y'know—it isn't much.

HAZEL. It's sixteen years ago——

ALAN. Seventeen.

HAZEL. Why, my Margaret's nearly as big as she was. Doesn't that seem strange, Kay ?

KAY. I'd nearly forgotten about Carol too.

MRS. CONWAY (*with some emotion*). Don't think I had—because I was so stupid about that grave. I'm not one of those people who remember graves, it's human beings I remember. Only the other day, when I was sitting upstairs, I heard Carol shouting, " Mo-ther, Mo-ther "—you know how she used to do. And then I began thinking about her, my poor darling, and how she came in that awful day, her face quite greyish, and said, " Mother, I've the most sickening pain," and then it was too late when they operated——

HAZEL. Yes, Mother, we remember.

ERNEST (*rising—harsh and astonishing*). I'll tell you what you don't remember—and what some of you never even knew. She was the best of the lot—that one—little Carol—worth all the rest of you put together.

HAZEL (*a shocked wife*). Ernest !

ERNEST. Yes, and I'm counting you in. You were the one I wanted—that's all right, I got the one I wanted—but it didn't

take me two hours to see that little Carol was the best of the lot.
(*He sits at the upstage end of the chesterfield and adds gloomily.*)
Didn't surprise me when she went off like that.   Out !   Finish !
Too good to last.

MRS. CONWAY (*now near to tears*).   Ernest is quite right.   She
was the best of you all.   My darling baby, I haven't forgotten
you, I haven't forgotten you.   (*Rising.*)   Oh, why isn't Robin
here ?   (*She begins weeping.*)   Go on, Gerald—explaining to
them.   I shan't be long.   Don't move.

(MRS. CONWAY *rises and goes out below the table, slightly luxurious
in her tears.   There is silence for a moment or two.*   MADGE
rises, comes to the table and sits L. *of it.*   ALAN *goes to the desk up* R.)

MADGE.   Surely under the circumstances it's absurd that
Mother and Alan should continue living in this house?   It's
much too large for them.

ALAN (*mildly*).   Yes.   We could do with something much
smaller now.

MADGE.   Then this house could be sold, that would help.
It's Mother's freehold, isn't it ?

GERALD.   Yes.   I think it would be better to move into
something smaller, just to cut down living expenses.   But this
house wouldn't fetch very much now.

HAZEL.   Why, Mother was offered thousands and thousands
for it just after the War.

ERNEST (*dryly*).   Yes, but this isn't just after the War.   It's
just before the next War.

GERALD.   How much do *you* think, Ernest ?

ERNEST.   Take anything you can get for it.

KAY.   Well, what are we supposed to do ?   If the worst
comes to the worst, we can club together to keep Mother
going——

MADGE.   But it's monstrous.   When I was at home—and
knew about things—we were considered quite well off.   There
were all the shares and property Father left, not simply for
Mother, but for all of us.   And now not only has it nearly
all been frittered away, but we're expected to provide for
Mother——

KAY (*rather wearily*).   But if the money's gone, it's gone.

GERALD.   No, the point is this——

(*He is stopped by three loud rings at the bell.   They turn and look
off* R.   ALAN *goes off and can be heard saying* " Good evening "
to ROBIN.   ROBIN *marches in.   He is wearing an old raincoat.
He is shabby with some traces of smartness, and looks what he is,
a slackish, hard-drinking, unsuccessful man of forty-two.*)

ROBIN (*as he enters*).   Everybody here ?
ALAN (*following him*).   Yes, all here.

ROBIN. Where's Mother ?
ALAN. She'll be back in a minute.

(ROBIN *takes off his raincoat and negligently gives it to* ALAN, *who characteristically accepts it and takes it off* R. ROBIN *takes no notice of this, but looks at* JOAN.)

ROBIN (*up* R.C.). Well, Joan. How are the offspring ?
JOAN (*stiffly*). They're quite well, Robin.
ROBIN. Still telling them what an awful man their father is ?
MADGE. Are we going to have this all over again ?
ROBIN. No, you're not—dear old Madge. Do I see a drink over there ? I do. (*He crosses to the small table up* L.) Have a drink, Gerald. Ernest, have a drink. No ? Well, I will.

(*He helps himself liberally to whisky and soda. After the first quick drink he turns, faces them and grins.* KAY *rises and touches him as she passes below* R. *of him to sit in the armchair above the fire.*)

Hello, Kay. Condescending to visit the provinces again, eh ?
KAY. Yes, but I've got to be back sometime to-night.
ROBIN. Don't blame you. Wish I was going back to town. That's the place. I've half a mind to chuck what I'm doing and try my luck there again. Know several decent chaps there.

(ALAN, *having taken* ROBIN'S *coat off, re-enters and sits on the window-seat.*)

KAY. What are you doing now, Robin ?
ROBIN (*dropping down* L.C. *with his drink—speaking rather gloomily*). Trying to sell a new heavy motor oil. I ought to have tried your stunt—writing. Might, one day. I could tell 'em something—my oath I could ! (*He finishes his drink rather noisily, looks at* JOAN, *who is still sitting on the pouffe by the fire, then crosses below the table to* R.C., *where he stands with his back to the audience. After a pause.*) Well, don't let me interrupt the business. Or are you waiting for Mother ?
MADGE. No, we're better without her.
ROBIN (*belligerently*). Yes, you would think that ! But don't forget, it's her money——

(ROBIN *stops because* MRS. CONWAY *reappears, all smiles.*)

MRS. CONWAY (*in the archway, joyfully*). Robin ! Now, this is nice !

(ROBIN *moves up to* L. *of her and she kisses him. There is perhaps a touch of defiance to the others in the warmth of her welcome.*)

Are you staying the night ?
ROBIN. I wasn't, but I could do—(*with a grin*)—in Alan's best pyjamas.

MADGE. We were just saying, Mother, that it was absurd
for you to keep on living here. The house is much too big
and expensive now.

ROBIN. That's for Mother to decide——

MRS. CONWAY. No, that's all right, dear. (*Sitting in the
chair* R. *of the table.*) It is too big now, and of course if I sold
it I could probably raise enough to convert the Church Road
houses into flats.

ERNEST. No, you couldn't. Nothing like.

MRS. CONWAY (*with dignity*). Really, Ernest! I was offered
five thousand pounds for it once.

ERNEST. You ought to have taken it.

GERALD. I'm afraid you can't count on getting much for this
house, though of course you'll save money by living in a smaller
place.

ROBIN (R. *of* GERALD). Not much, though. She'd have to
pay rent for the smaller house, and this is hers.

(GERALD *ignores him, and he crosses above* GERALD *to the small
table up* L. *for another drink.*)

GERALD. But rates and taxes are fairly heavy on this house.
I want you all to understand that the present situation is very
unsatisfactory. The overdraft can be paid off, of course, simply
by selling shares or some of the houses, but after that Mrs.
Conway would be worse off than ever. If the money for the
conversion scheme could be raised, then the Church Road
property would bring in a decent income.

MRS. CONWAY. And I'm sure that's the thing to do. Flats.
I might live in one of them myself—a nice, cosy little flat.
Delightful!

GERALD. But after you've sold your shares you've still to
find another two or three thousand to pay for the conversion
into flats.

MRS. CONWAY. But couldn't I borrow that?

GERALD. Not from the bank. They won't accept the Church
Road houses as security for a loan to convert them into flats.
I've tried that.

HAZEL (*hopefully, and a shade timidly*). Ernest—could lend
you the money?

ERNEST (*rising—staggered by this*). What!

HAZEL (*rather faltering now*). Well, you could easily afford it,
Ernest.

MRS. CONWAY (*smiling*). From what I hear, you're very well
off indeed these days, Ernest.

GERALD. Oh—there's no doubt about that.

MRS. CONWAY (*hoping this will win him over*). And it only
seems yesterday, Ernest, that you first came here—a very shy
young man from nowhere.

ERNEST (R.C., *grimly*). It's twenty years ago—but that's just what I was—a shy young man from nowhere. And when I managed to wangle myself into this house, I thought I'd got somewhere.

MRS. CONWAY. I remember so well feeling that about you at the time, Ernest.

ERNEST. Yes. I was made to feel I'd got somewhere, too. But I stuck it. I've always been able to stick it when I've had my mind on something I badly wanted. That's how I've managed to get on.

ROBIN (*who doesn't like him, obviously*). Don't begin to tell us now that you landed here with only a shilling in your pocket

———

MRS. CONWAY (*warning, reproachful, yet secretly amused*). Now, now, Robin !

ERNEST (*in level, unpleasant tone*). I wasn't going to. Don't worry, you're not going to have the story of *my* life. All I was about to say was—that as far as I'm concerned, you can whistle for your two or three thousand pounds. You won't get a penny from me. And I might as well tell you—while I'm making myself unpleasant—that I could lend you the two or three thousand without feeling it. Only, I'm not going to. Not a penny.

HAZEL (*indignation struggling with her fear of him*). You make me feel ashamed.

ERNEST (*staring hard at her*). Oh ! Why ?

HAZEL *does not reply, but begins to crumple under his hard stare.*)

Go on. Tell 'em why I make you feel ashamed. Tell *me*. Or would you like to tell me later when *I'm* telling *you* a few things ?

(HAZEL *crumples into tears.* ROBIN *comes to* L. *of the table, between* GERALD *and* MADGE.)

ROBIN (*furious*). I never did like you, Beevers. I've half a mind to boot you out of this house.

ERNEST (*no coward*). You do, and I'll bring an action for assault. *And* I'd enjoy it. My money or the boot, eh ? I told Hazel a long time ago that not one of you would ever get a penny out of me. And I'm not mean. Ask her. But I swore to myself after the very first night I came here, when you were all being so high and mighty—especially you—that you'd never see a penny that I ever made.

ROBIN (*with a lurking grin, turning up stage*). I see.

ERNEST (*very sharply*). What's that mean ? By God, she *has* ! She's been giving you money—*my* money.

HAZEL (*rising—terribly alarmed now*). Oh—Robin, you shouldn't——

ROBIN (*up* L.C.—*irritably*). What does it matter ? He can't eat you.

ERNEST (*very quiet and deadly, to* HAZEL). Come on.

(*He exits.* HAZEL *looks terrified.*)

MADGE. Don't go, if you don't want to.

KAY. Hazel, there's nothing to be afraid of.

HAZEL (*sincere, quiet, desperate*). There is. I'm frightened of *him*. Except right at the first—I've always been frightened of him.

ROBIN (*noisily, coming down* L. *towards* HAZEL). Don't be silly. That little pipsqueak! What can *he* do?

HAZEL. I don't know. It isn't that. It's just something about him.

(ERNEST *reappears in the archway buttoning up his overcoat.*)

ERNEST (*to* HAZEL, *as if they were alone*). Come on. I'm going.

HAZEL (*summoning up all her courage*). N-no.

(*He waits and looks at her.* MRS. CONWAY *rises and goes up to*
L. *of* ERNEST.)

MRS. CONWAY (*excitedly*). You sneaked your way in here, Ernest Beevers, and somehow you persuaded or bullied Hazel, who was considered then one of the prettiest girls in Newlingham, into marrying you——

HAZEL (*moving to below the table* C.—*imploring her*). No, Mother—please don't——

MRS. CONWAY. I'll tell him now what I've always wanted to tell him. (*Approaching* ERNEST *and speaking with vehemence.*) I was a fool. My husband wouldn't have had such a bullying, mean little rat near the house. I never liked you. And I'm not surprised to hear you say you've always hated us. Don't ever come here again, don't ever let me see you again. I only wish I was Hazel for just one day, I'd show you something. What—you—my daughter——! (*In a sudden fury, she slaps him hard across the face. With a certain grand magnificence of manner.*) Now bring an action for that! (*She stands there, blazing at him.*)

(ERNEST *rubs his cheek a little, looking at her steadily.*)

ERNEST (*quietly*). You've done a lot of dam' silly things in your time, Mrs. Conway, but you'll find that's the dam' silliest. (*To* HAZEL.) Come on.

(ERNEST *goes out.* HAZEL *is wretched.*)

HAZEL. Oh—Mother—you shouldn't——

ROBIN (L.C., *rather grandly*). She did quite right. And you just let me know—if he gives you any trouble.

HAZEL (*tearfully, shaking her head, as she wanders towards the archway*). No, Robin. You don't understand . . . you don't understand . . .

(HAZEL *goes out slowly. The front door is heard shutting. There is a strained silence.* MRS. CONWAY *goes back to sit* R. *of the table.* ROBIN *goes to the small table up* L.)

MRS. CONWAY (*with a short laugh*). Well—I suppose that was a silly thing to do——

GERALD (*gravely*). I'm afraid it was, y'know. (*He rises and goes to the desk up* R. *to put his papers in his case.*)

KAY (*rather painfully, rising and going up to the window-seat*). You see, it's Hazel who will have to pay for it.

ROBIN (*pouring himself another drink*). Well, she needn't. She's only to let me know what he's up to.

JOAN (*surprisingly*). What's the good of talking like that—— What could *you* do ? He can make her life a misery, and you couldn't stop it.

MADGE. Well, it's her own fault. I've no patience with her. I wouldn't stand it ten minutes.

JOAN (*with plenty of spirit, for her*). It's no use you talking, Madge. You simply don't understand. You've never been married.

MADGE. No, and after what I've seen here I think I'm lucky.

MRS. CONWAY (*with energy*). You're not lucky—never were and never will be—and as you haven't the least idea what a woman's real life is like, the less you say, the better. You're not among schoolgirls and silly teachers now. Robin, give me a glass of port. Won't you have a drink too ?

(ROBIN *pours her a port.*)

GERALD (*who has put his papers away in his case*). I don't think there's any point in my staying any longer.

MRS. CONWAY. But we haven't settled anything.

GERALD (*dropping down* R.C. *and speaking rather coldly*). I thought there was a chance that Ernest Beevers might have been persuaded to lend you the money. As I don't think anybody else here has three thousand pounds to spare——

(ROBIN, *who has come to* L. *of the table* C. *to pass the glass of port across to* MRS. CONWAY, *turns on him.*)

ROBIN. All right, Thornton, you needn't be so damned super-cilious about it. Seems to me you've not made a particularly bright job of handling my mother's affairs——

GERALD (*annoyed*). I don't think that comes too well from you. For years I've given good advice, and never once has it been acted upon. Now I'd be only too delighted to hand over these affairs.

ROBIN (*going back to the small table up* L.). I believe I could make a better job of it myself.

GERALD (*stiffly*). I can't imagine a possibly worse choice. Good night, Mrs. Conway. (*He shakes hands with her, then moves with his case.*) Good night, Kay. Good night, Alan——

(*He exits, followed by* ALAN.)

JOAN (*rising and going below the table to the archway*). I think I'll come along too, Gerald.

ROBIN (*dropping down a little* L.C.). You'll be able to have a nice little chat about me on the way.

JOAN (*turning at the archway*). It doesn't hurt as much as it used to do, Robin, when you talk so bitterly. I suppose one day it won't hurt at all.

ROBIN (*who is sorry, at the moment*). Sorry, old girl. And give my love to the kids. Say I'm coming to see them soon.

JOAN. Yes, come and see us soon. Only remember—we're very poor now.

ROBIN. Thanks for that. And then you talk about being bitter.

(*They look at one another for a moment, lost and hopeless. Then* JOAN *moves away, slowly.* ROBIN *returns to the table up* L.)

KAY (*dropping down to* L. *of* JOAN—*rather painfully*). Good night, my dear.

JOAN (*painfully turning and producing a little social smile*). Good night, Kay. It's been nice—seeing you again.

(JOAN *kisses her and goes.* KAY, *who is moved, sits on the chesterfield* R. ROBIN *comes to* L. *of the table* C.)

ROBIN (*after another drink, an optimist*). Well, now we ought to be able to settle something——

MADGE (*coldly, rising and going to the fireplace to light a cigarette*). So far as I'm concerned, this has simply been a waste of time—and nervous energy.

MRS. CONWAY (*with malice*). You know, Madge, when I think of Gerald Thornton as he is now, a dreary, conceited middle-aged bachelor, I can't help thinking it's perhaps a pity you *didn't* marry him.

ROBIN (*with a roar, sitting in the chair* L. *of the table with his back to the audience*). What, Madge ! I never knew she fancied Gerald Thornton.

MRS. CONWAY (*in a light but significant tone*). She did—once. Didn't you, dear ? And I believe he was interested. Oh, a long time ago, when you children were all still at home.

KAY (*rather sharply*). Mother, if that's not true, then it's stupid, silly talk. If it *is* true, then it's cruel.

MRS. CONWAY. Nonsense! And not so high-and-mighty—please—Kay.

MADGE (*turning at the fireplace and speaking very quietly*). It *was* true, a long time ago, just after the War. When I still thought we could suddenly make everything better for everybody. Socialism! Peace! Universal brotherhood! All that. And I felt then that Gerald Thornton and I together could—help. He had a lot of fine qualities, I thought—I believe he had then, too—and only needed to be pulled out of his rut here, to have his enthusiasm aroused. I was remembering to-night—when I was looking at him. It came back to me quite quickly. (*This last was more to* KAY *than the other two. Now she takes her mother in.*) One evening—just one evening—and something you did that evening—ruined it all. I'd almost forgotten—but seeing us all here again to-night reminded me—I believe it was at a sort of party for you, Kay. (*Accusingly to her mother.*) Do you remember?

MRS. CONWAY. Really, Madge, you *are* absurd. I seem to remember some piece of nonsense, when we were all being foolish.

MADGE. Yes, you remember. It was quite deliberate on your part. Just to keep a useful young man unattached or jealousy of a girl's possible happiness or just out of sheer nasty female mischief. . . . And something went for ever. . . .

MRS. CONWAY. It can't have been worth very much, then.

MADGE (*turning to put her cigarette out in the ash-tray on the mantelpiece*). A seed is easily destroyed, but it might have grown into an oak tree. (*Turning back to her mother with great emotion.*) I'm glad I'm not a mother.

MRS. CONWAY. Yes, you may well say that.

MADGE. I know how I'd have despised myself if I'd turned out to be a bad mother.

MRS. CONWAY (*angrily, rising* R.C.). So that's what you call me? (*She pauses, then with more vehemence and emotion.*) Just because you never think of anybody but yourselves. All selfish—selfish. Because everything hasn't happened as you wanted it, turn on me—all my fault. You never really think about me. Don't try to see things for a moment from my point of view. When you were children, I was so proud of you all, so confident that you would grow up to be wonderful creatures. I used to see myself at the age I am now, surrounded by you and your own children, so proud of you, so happy with you all, this house happier and gayer even than it was in the best of the old days. And now my life's gone by, and what's happened? You're a resentful soured schoolmistress, middle-aged before your time. Hazel—the loveliest child there ever was—married to a vulgar little bully, and terrified of him. (*Turning to* KAY.) Kay here gone away to lead her own life, and very bitter and secretive

about it, as if she'd failed. (*Turning up stage a few steps.*) Carol
—the happiest and kindest of you all—dead before she's twenty.
(*Above the table and* R. *of it.*) Robin—I know, my dear, I'm not
blaming you now, but I must speak the truth for once—with a
wife he can't love and no sort of position or comfort or anything.
And Alan—the eldest, the boy his father adored, that he thought
might do anything—what's he now ?

(ALAN *has come in now and is standing quietly in the archway.*)

A miserable clerk with no prospects, no ambition, no self-respect,
a shabby man that nobody would look at twice. (*She sees him
standing there now, but in her worked-up fury does not care, and
lashes out at him.*) Yes, a shabby little clerk that nobody would
look at twice.

(KAY *rises and goes up to* R. *of* ALAN, *between him and* MRS.
CONWAY.)

KAY (*in a sudden fury of loyalty*). How dare you, Mother,
how dare you ! Alan of all people !
ALAN (*with a smile*). That's all right, Kay. Don't you get
excited. It's not a bad description. I am a shabby little clerk,
y'know. It must be very disappointing——

(ALAN *and* KAY *exchange a sympathetic smile, then* KAY *sits on
the chesterfield again.* ALAN *remains just above it and later
drifts to the desk up* R.)

MRS. CONWAY. Oh—don't be so forgiving ! Robin, you've
always been selfish and weak and a bit of a good-for-nothing——
ROBIN (*rising and going above the table to* L. *of* MRS. CONWAY,
R.C.). Here, steady, old girl. I've had some rotten bad luck,
too, y'know, and a lot of it's just luck. I've come to see that.
MRS. CONWAY (*exhausted now*). All right—add the bad luck
too, my dear. The point is, whatever they may say about you,
Robin, my darling, you're my own boy and my own sort, and a
great comfort. So you and I will go upstairs and talk.
ROBIN (*as she takes his arm*). That's the spirit !

(*They move together towards the arch.*)

MADGE (*at the fire—very quietly*). Mother !

(MRS. CONWAY *stops, but does not turn.* MADGE *comes to* L. *of the
table.*)

We've both said what we want to say. There isn't any more
to be said. And if you decide to have any more of these family
conferences, don't trouble to ask me to attend them, because I
shan't. I don't expect now to see a penny of father's money.
And please don't expect to see any of mine.
ROBIN. Who wants yours ?

Mrs. Conway. Come on, my dear, and we'll talk like human beings.

(*They go out.* Madge *picks up her bag from* l. *of the table and goes to the fireplace for her cigarette-case which she has left on the mantelpiece.*)

Madge. I have an idea I wasn't too pleasant to you, Kay, earlier when we met to-night. If so, I'm sorry.

Kay. That's all right, Madge. Are you going back to Collingfield to-night ?

Madge. No, I can't. But I'm staying with Nora Fleming—you remember her ? (*She crosses below the table to* r.c.) She's Head of Newlingham High now. I've left my things there. I'll go now. I don't want to see Mother again.

Kay (*rising to* r. *of her*). Good-bye, Madge. I hope you collar one of these headships. (*She kisses her.*)

Madge. Good-bye, Kay. And do try and write a good book, instead of doing nothing but this useless journalism.

(Madge *goes off, followed by* Alan. Kay, *left to herself, shows that she is deeply moved. She wanders about restlessly. She switches off the chandelier at the switch below the arch, which leaves only the brackets at the fireplace. She crosses above the table* c. *to the small table up* l., *hastily pours herself a whisky and soda and brings it down to the fireplace. She lights a cigarette, tastes the whisky, then, ignoring the cigarette and the whisky, stares into the past. Leaning on the mantelpiece she softly begins to cry.* Alan *returns, filling his pipe, and comes to below the table.*)

Alan (*cheerfully*). You've a good half-hour yet, Kay, before you need set out for the London train. I'll take you to the station. (*He comes up to* r. *of her.*) What's the matter ? Has all this—been a bit too much for you ?

Kay (*ruefully*). Apparently. And I thought I was tough now, Alan. Look, I was doing the modern working woman—a cigarette and a whisky and soda . . . no good, though . . . (*Sitting in the armchair above the fireplace.*) You see, Alan, I've not only been here to-night, I've been here remembering, other nights, long ago, when we weren't like this . . .

Alan (*slowly, not eagerly*). Yes, I know—those old Christmas and birthday parties. (*He turns the chair* l. *of the table and sits facing her.*)

Kay (*half smiling, but deeply moved*). Yes, I remembered. I saw all of us then. Myself too. Oh, silly girl of nineteen-nineteen ! Oh, lucky girl !

Alan. You mustn't mind, too much. It's all right, y'know. Like being forty ?

Kay. Oh no, Alan, it's hideous and unbearable. Remember

what we once were and what we thought we'd be. And now this. And it's all we have, Alan, it's *us*. Every step we've taken—every tick of the clock—making everything worse. If this is all life is, what's the use ? Better to die, like Carol, before you find it out, before Time gets to work on you. I've felt it before, Alan, but never as I've done to-night. There's a great devil in the universe, and we call it Time.

ALAN (*playing with his pipe, quietly, shyly*).　Did you ever read Blake ?

KAY.　Yes.

ALAN.　Do you remember this ?　(*He quotes, quietly but with feeling.*)

> Joy and woe are woven fine,
> A clothing for the soul divine ;
> Under every grief and pine
> Runs a joy with silken twine.
> It is right it should be so ;
> Man was made for joy and woe ;
> And when this we rightly know,
> Safely through the world we go. . . .

KAY.　Safely through the world we go ?　No, it isn't true, Alan—or it isn't true for me. If things were merely mixed—good and bad—that would be all right, but they get worse. We've seen it to-night. Time's beating us.

ALAN.　No, Time's only a kind of dream, Kay. If it wasn't, it would have to destroy everything—the whole universe—and then remake it again every tenth of a second. But Time doesn't destroy anything. It merely moves us on—in this life—from one peephole to the next.

KAY.　But the happy young Conways, who used to play charades here, they've gone, and gone for ever.

ALAN.　No, they're real and existing, just as we two, here now, are real and existing. We're seeing another bit of the view—a bad bit, if you like—but the whole landscape's still there.

KAY.　But, Alan, we can't be anything but what we are *now*.

ALAN.　It's hard to explain . . . suddenly like this . . . there's a book I'll lend you—read it in the train. But the point is, now, at this moment, or any moment, we're only a cross-section of our real selves. What we *really* are is the whole stretch of ourselves, all our time, and when we come to the end of this life, all those selves, all our time, will be *us*—the real you, the real me. And then perhaps we'll find ourselves in another time, which is only another kind of dream.

KAY.　I'll try to understand . . . so long as you really believe—and think it's possible for me to believe—that Time's not ticking our lives away . . . wrecking . . . and ruining everything . . . for ever . . .

ALAN. It's all right, Kay. (*He leans forward and puts his hand on hers.*) I'll get you that book. (*He rises and goes between his chair and hers above the table towards the arch, but turns to her above the table.*) I believe half our trouble now is because we think Time's ticking our lives away. That's why we snatch and grab and hurt each other.

KAY. As if we were all in a panic on a sinking ship.

ALAN. Yes, like that.

KAY. But you don't do those things—bless you !

ALAN. I think it's easier not to—if you take a long view.

KAY. As if we're—immortal beings ?

ALAN (*smiling*). Yes, and in for a tremendous adventure.

(ALAN *goes out.* KAY, *comforted but brooding, goes up to the window, parts the curtains and stands looking off towards* L.)

CURTAIN.

ACT III

SCENE.—*The same as Act I. The evening of the party again. The room and everything in it is exactly as it was at the end of Act I.* KAY *is sitting exactly as she was, in the window, and is listening to* MRS. CONWAY *singing the second half of Schumann's " Der Nussbaum." She keeps still until the song is done. Something—vague, elusive, a brief vision, a presentiment—is haunting her. She stares at nothing, as if trying to recapture something. She looks vaguely disturbed, frowns, and tries to shake something off.*

When the song is ended there is some applause off. ALAN *enters and switches on the chandelier and standard lamp at the switches below the archway.* KAY *looks at him, puzzled. He grins and rubs his hands a little.*

ALAN. Well, Kay ?

(KAY *rises and comes down to* L. *of him, up* R.C.)

KAY (*as if to break into something important*). Alan—— (*Breaks off.*)

ALAN. Yes ?

KAY (*hurriedly*). No—nothing.

(*He looks closer at her.*)

ALAN. I believe you've been asleep—while Mother was singing.

KAY (*rather confusedly*). No. I was sitting here—listening. I turned the light out. (*Slowly.*) No, I didn't fall asleep. I don't know, though. Perhaps I did—just for a second. It couldn't have been longer.

ALAN. But you'd know if you'd been asleep.

KAY. No, I wasn't asleep—but quite suddenly—I thought I saw . . . we were—anyhow, I'm sure you came into it, Alan.

ALAN. Came into what ?

KAY. I can't remember, but I know I was listening to Mother singing all the time—and I'm—a bit—wuzzy.

(*Voices off. Some " Good nights," etc.*)

ALAN (*below the table up* R.). Most of the people are going now. You'd better go and say good night.

(HAZEL *enters, carrying a plate on which is an enormous piece of sticky, rich, creamy cake. She has already begun to tackle this as she moves in. She crosses below* KAY *and* ALAN *to the chesterfield* L.)

KAY (*seeing her*). Hazel, you greedy pig ! (*She deftly swoops up a bit of the cake and eats it.*)

HAZEL (*talking with her mouth rather full*). I didn't come in here just to eat this. (*She sits on the* R. *arm of the chesterfield.*)

KAY. 'Course you did !

HAZEL. They're all saying good night now, and I'm dodging that little horror Gerald Thornton brought.

KAY (*hastily*). I must say my piece to them.

(KAY *hurries off.* ALAN *lingers below the table up* R.)

ALAN (*after a pause, moving to* R. *of her*). Hazel !

HAZEL (*with her mouth full*). Um ?

ALAN (*with an elaborate air of casualness*). What's Joan Helford going to do now ?

HAZEL. Oh—just mooch round a bit.

ALAN. I thought I heard her saying she was going away—I was wondering if she was leaving Newlingham.

HAZEL. She's only going to stay with her aunt. Joan's always staying with aunts. Why can't *we* have aunts planted all over the place ?

ALAN. There's Aunt Edith.

HAZEL (*the height of scorn*). And a doctor's house in Wolverhampton ! Ghastly ! (*With quick change of tone—teasingly.*) Anything else you'd like to know about Joan ?

ALAN (*confused*). No—no. I—just wondered.

(*He turns up towards the window and almost bumps into* ERNEST, *who is wearing a very shabby mackintosh-raincoat and carrying a bowler hat. As soon as* HAZEL *sees who it is, she rises and turns away and has another dab at her cake.* ALAN *stops, and so does* ERNEST. *Voices off. More* " Good nights," *etc.*)

Oh !—you going ?

ERNEST (*a man who knows his own mind*). In a minute. (*He is standing below the table up* R. *and is obviously waiting for* ALAN *to clear out.*)

ALAN (*rather confused*). Yes—well—— (*He makes a move and crosses below* ERNEST *to the downstage corner of the arch.*)

HAZEL (L.C. *below the chesterfield, loudly and clearly*). Alan, you're not going ?

(*She looks across, completely ignoring* ERNEST, *who waits, not perhaps quite as cool as he would appear on the surface, for the hat he is clutching moves a bit.*)

ALAN (*not at home in this*). Yes—have to say good night and get their coats and things—you know——

(ALAN *goes out. The voices off cease.* HAZEL *attends to her cake and then looks, without a smile, at* ERNEST.)

ERNEST (*moving in a little to above the ottoman*). I just looked in to say good night, Miss Conway.

HAZEL (*blankly*). Oh—yes—of course. Well——

ERNEST (*cutting in*). It's been a great pleasure to me to come here and meet you all.

(*He waits a moment. She finds herself compelled to speak.*)

HAZEL (*in the same tone*). Oh—well——

ERNEST (*cutting in again as he moves to* C.). Especially you. I'm new round here, y'know. I've only been in the place about three months. I bought a share in that paper mill—Eckersley's —out at West Newlingham—you know it ?

HAZEL (*no encouragement from her*). No.

ERNEST. Thought you might have noticed it. Been there long enough. Matter of fact it wants rebuilding. But that's where I am. And I hadn't been here a week before I noticed you, Miss Conway.

HAZEL (*who knows it only too well*). Did you ?

ERNEST. Yes. And I've been watching out for you ever since. I expect you've noticed me knocking about.

HAZEL (*loftily*). No, I don't think I have.

ERNEST (*moving towards her*). Oh—yes—you must have done. Come on, now. Admit it.

HAZEL (*her natural self coming out now*). Well, if you must know, I *have* noticed you——

ERNEST (*pleased*). I thought so.

HAZEL (*rapidly and indignantly*). Because I thought you behaved very stupidly and rudely. If you want to look silly yourself—that's your affair—but you'd no right to make me look silly too——

ERNEST (*rather crushed*). Oh ! I didn't know—it'ud been as bad as that——

HAZEL (*feeling she has the upper hand*). Well, it has.

(*He stares at her, perhaps having moved a little closer. She does not look at him at first, but then is compelled to meet his hard stare. There is something about this look that penetrates to the essential weakness of her character.*)

ERNEST (*coming up again now*). I'm sorry. Though I can't see anybody's much the worse for it. After all, we've only one life to live, let's get on with it, I say. And in my opinion, you're the best-looking girl in this town, Miss Hazel Conway.

(HAZEL *moves away to the fireplace.*)

I've been telling you that—in my mind—for the last two months. But I knew it wouldn't be long before I got to know you. To tell you properly.

(ERNEST *looks hard at her. She does not like him, but is completely helpless before this direct attack. He nods slowly.*)

I expect you're thinking I'm not much of a chap. But there's a bit more in me than meets the eye. A few people have found that out already, and a lot more'll find it out before so long— here in Newlingham. You'll see. (*He changes his tone now, because he is uncertain on purely social matters—almost humbly.*) Would it be all right—if I—sort of—called to see you—some time soon ?

HAZEL (*crossing below him and above the ottoman to below the table up* R.). You'd better ask my mother.

ERNEST (*below the chesterfield, jocularly*). Oh !—sort of *Ask Mamma* business, eh ?

HAZEL (*confused and annoyed*). No—I didn't mean it like that at all. I meant that this is Mother's house——

ERNEST. Yes, but you're old enough now to have your own friends, aren't you ?

HAZEL (*dropping down* R.C. *between the ottoman and the desk*). I don't make friends with people very quickly.

ERNEST (*with appalling bluntness, moving* C.). Oh ! I'd heard you did.

HAZEL (*haughtily and angrily*). Do you mean to say you've been discussing me with people ?

ERNEST. Yes. Why not ?

(*They stare at each other.* ERNEST *coolly and deliberately, and* HAZEL *with attempted hauteur.* HAZEL *sits on* R. *side of the ottoman, when* MADGE *and* ROBIN *enter together, in the middle of a talk.*)

MADGE (*off stage*). But, Robin, you don't mean to say you actually did their work for them ?

(ROBIN *comes in first and crosses above* ERNEST *to the fireplace* L. MADGE *follows to above the chesterfield.*)

ROBIN (*who is in great form*). Golly yes ! It was a great lark. We weren't in uniform, y'know. I did some stoking. Hard work, but a great stunt.

MADGE (*hotly*). It wasn't. You ought to have been ashamed of yourselves.

ROBIN (*surprised*). Why ? (*He sits on the* L. *arm of the chester-field, with his feet up.*)

(ERNEST, *left thus, has wondered whether to go or not, but eventually comes to* R. *end of the chesterfield to listen to* MADGE'S *argument.*)

MADGE (*above the chesterfield—with vehemence*). Because helping to break a strike and being a blackleg isn't a lark and a stunt. Those railwaymen were desperately anxious to improve their conditions. They didn't go on strike for fun. It was a very serious thing for them and for their wives and families. And then people like you, Robin, think it's amusing when you try to do their work and make the strike useless. I think it's shameful the way the middle classes turn against the working class.

ROBIN (*rather out of his depth now*). But there had to be some sort of train service.

MADGE. Why ? If the public had to do without trains altogether, they might realize then that the railwaymen have some grievances.

ERNEST (*sardonically*). They might. But I've an idea they'd be too busy with their own grievance—no trains. And you only want a few more railway strikes and then half their traffic will be gone for ever, turned into road transport. And what do your clever railwaymen do then ? (*He pauses.*)

(MADGE *is listening, of course, but not quite acknowledging that he had any right to join in. She is about to reply when* ERNEST *continues.*)

And another thing. The working class is out for itself. Then why shouldn't the middle class be out for itself ?

MADGE (*coldly*). Because the middle class must have already been " out for itself "—as you call it——

ERNEST. Well, what do you call it ? Something in Latin ?

(MADGE *goes round above the chesterfield and comes down* L. *of it.*)

MADGE (*with chill impatience*). I say the middle class must have already been successfully out for itself or it wouldn't be a comfortable middle class. Then why turn against the working class when at last it tries to look after itself ?

ERNEST (*cynically*). That's easy. There's only so much to go round, and if you take more, then I get less.

MADGE (*standing on the low footstool by the fire—rather sharply*). I'm sorry, but that's bad economics as well as bad ethics.

ROBIN (*bursting out*). But we'd have Red Revolution—like Russia—if we began to listen to these wild chaps like——

HAZEL (*rising and moving to the archway*). Well, I think it's all silly. Why can't people agree ?

ERNEST (*seeing her going, and crossing towards* L. *of her*). Oh ! —Miss Conway——

HAZEL (*her very blank sweetness a snub*). Oh—yes—— Good night.

(HAZEL *goes out.* ERNEST *looks after her, a rather miserable figure. Then he looks towards* ROBIN *just in time to catch a grin on his face before it is almost—but not quite—wiped off.* MADGE *crosses below* ERNEST *and above the ottoman towards the archway.*)

MADGE (*to* ROBIN). I came in here for something. What was it? (*She looks about her and through* ERNEST, *whom she obviously dislikes.*)

ROBIN (*still a grin lurking*). Don't ask me.

(MADGE *finds her copy of "The Nation" on the chair above the desk and goes, ignoring* ERNEST, *though more absently than pointedly.* ROBIN, *still looking vaguely mocking, looks for a match on the mantelpiece, crosses* R. *below the ottoman to look on the desk, then goes to the table up* R. *where he finds one and lights a cigarette.*)

(*Casually.*) Were you in the army?

ERNEST (L. *of him*). Yes. Two years.

ROBIN. What crush?

ERNEST. Army Pay Corps.

ROBIN (*easily, not too rudely*). That must have been fun for you.

(ERNEST *looks as if he is going to make an angry retort, but crosses to below* R. *end of the chesterfield when* CAROL *hurries in.*)

CAROL (*in the archway*). Mr. Beevers——

(*As he turns, looking rather sullen,* ROBIN *wanders out.*)

(*Crossing to* R. *of him.*) Oh!—you look *put out.*

ERNEST (*grimly*). That's about it. Put out!

CAROL (*looking hard at him*). I believe you're all hot and angry inside, aren't you?

ERNEST (*taking it as lightly as he can*). Or disappointed. Which is it?

CAROL. A mixture, I expect. Well, Mr. Beevers, you mustn't. You were very nice about the charade—and very good in it, too—and I don't suppose you've ever played before, have you?

ERNEST. No. (*Grimly.*) They didn't go in for those sort of things in my family.

CAROL (*looking at him critically*). No, I don't think you've had enough fun. That's your trouble, Mr. Beevers. You must come and play charades again.

ERNEST (*as if setting her apart from the others*). *You're* all right, y'know.

(MRS. CONWAY'S *voice, very clear, is heard off saying :* " But surely he's gone, hasn't he? ")

CAROL (*with a sort of quaint wisdom*). We're *all* all right, you know. And don't forget that, Mr. Beevers.

ERNEST (*liking her*). You're a funny kid.

CAROL (*severely*). I'm not very funny and I'm certainly not a kid——

ERNEST. Oh—sorry!

CAROL (*serenely*). I'll forgive you this time.

(MRS. CONWAY *enters with* GERALD. *She looks rather surprised to see* ERNEST *still there. He notices this.*)

ERNEST (*awkwardly, crossing above the ottoman to* L. *of her*). I'm just going, Mrs. Conway. (*To* GERALD.) You coming along?

MRS. CONWAY (*smoothly but quickly, moving to* R. *of* GERALD, *who is below the table up* R.). No, Mr. Thornton and I want to talk business for a few minutes.

ERNEST. I see. Well, good night, Mrs. Conway. (*Shaking hands with her.*) And I'm very pleased to have met you.

MRS. CONWAY (*condescendingly gracious*). Good night, Mr. Beevers. Carol, will you——

CAROL (*cheerfully*). Yes.

(*She crosses above the ottoman to* ERNEST, *claps him on the back and speaks in imitation Western American accent.* ERNEST *looks rather bewildered by it.*)

I'll set you and your hoss on the big trail, pardner.

(CAROL *and* ERNEST *go out.* MRS. CONWAY *and* GERALD *watch them go. Then* GERALD *turns and raises his eyebrows at her.* MRS. CONWAY *shakes her head.* GERALD *crosses to below* L. *end of the chesterfield.* MRS. CONWAY *takes the cigarette-box from the table up* R., *brings it* L. *and offers* GERALD *a cigarette. He takes one and she puts the box down on the table above the chesterfield.*)

MRS. CONWAY (*briskly*). I'm sorry if your little friend thought he was being pushed out, but really, Gerald, the children would never have forgiven me if I'd encouraged him to stay any longer.

GERALD. I'm afraid Beevers hasn't been a success.

MRS. CONWAY (*sitting* R. *on the chesterfield*). Well, after all, he is—rather—isn't he?

GERALD. I did warn you, y'know. And really he was so desperately keen to meet the famous Conways.——

MRS. CONWAY. Hazel, you mean.

GERALD. Hazel, especially, but he was determined to know the whole family.

MRS. CONWAY. Well, I do think they're an attractive lot of children.

GERALD (*sitting* L. *of her on the chesterfield*). Only outshone by their attractive mother.

MRS. CONWAY (*delighted*) Gerald! I believe you're going to flirt with me.

GERALD. Of course I am. By the way, there *wasn't* any business you wanted to discuss, was there?

MRS. CONWAY. No, not really. But I think you ought to know I've had another *enormous* offer for this house. Of course, I wouldn't dream of selling it, but it's nice to know it's worth so much. Oh!—and young George Farrow would like me to sell him my share in the firm, and says he's ready to make an offer that would surprise me.

GERALD. I believe it would be pretty handsome too. But of course there's no point in selling out when they're paying fifteen per cent. And once we're really out of this war-time atmosphere and the government restrictions are off, there's going to be a tremendous boom.

MRS. CONWAY. Isn't that lovely? All the children back home, and plenty of money to help them to settle down. And, mind you, Gerald, I shouldn't be a bit surprised if Robin doesn't do awfully well in some business quite soon. *Selling* things, probably—people find him so attractive. Dear Robin! (*She pauses, then continues with a change of tone, more depth, feeling.*) Gerald, it isn't so very long ago that I thought myself the unluckiest woman in the world. If it hadn't been for the children, I wouldn't have wanted to go on living. Sometimes—without *him*—I didn't want to go on living. And now—though of course it'll never be the same without *him*—I suddenly feel I'm one of the luckiest women in the world. All my children round me, quite safe at last, very happy——

(ROBIN'S *voice, shouting, off:* " It's hide-and-seek all over the house.")

Did he say " all over the house "?

GERALD. Yes.

MRS. CONWAY (*calling*). Not in my room, Robin, please.

ROBIN'S VOICE (*off, shouting*). Mother's room's barred.

JOAN'S VOICE (*farther off, shouting*). Who's going to be It?

ROBIN'S VOICE (*off*). I am. Mother, come on. Where's Gerald?

MRS. CONWAY (*as she rises and moves above the ottoman towards the archway, followed by* GERALD). Just to hear him shouting about the house again—you don't know what it means to me, Gerald. And you never will know.

(*They go out.*)

ROBIN'S VOICE (*loud, off*). I'll go into the coat cupboard and count fifty. Now then—scatter, everybody. Shush!

(After a moment JOAN *enters, happy and breathless. She switches off the chandelier from the switch downstage of the arch, leaving only the* L. *half of the stage illuminated by the standard lamp. After looking about she chooses a hiding-place—kneeling behind* L. *end of the chesterfield. No sooner has she installed herself than* ALAN *enters and moves across to* R. *end of the chesterfield. She peeps out and sees him.)*

JOAN *(imploring whisper).* Oh—Alan—don't hide in here.

ALAN *(humbly).* I came specially. I saw you come in.

JOAN. No, please. Go somewhere else.

ALAN *(wistfully).* You look so pretty, Joan.

JOAN. Do I ? That's sweet of you, Alan.

ALAN. Can I stay, then ?

JOAN. No, please. It's *so* much more fun if you go somewhere else. Alan, don't spoil it.

ALAN *(rather miserably).* Spoil what ?

JOAN *(very hurriedly).* The game—of course. *(She rises and crosses to him, leading him towards the arch.)* Go on, Alan, there's a pet.

ROBIN *(off).* Forty-nine . . . Fifty ! !

JOAN. Oh—you can't go out that way now. You'll have to go out of the window and then round. (R. *of him, pushing him towards the window.)* Go on.

ALAN. All right.

(He gets out of the window.)

(Softly, looking in from L. *of the window.)* Good-bye, Joan.

JOAN (R. *of the window, whispering).* Why do you say that ?

ALAN *(very sadly).* Because I feel it *is* good-bye.

(He disappears towards L. JOAN *hurries back to her hiding-place.* ROBIN's *voice, humming, is heard off. Then half humming, half singing, a popular song of the period, " If you were the only girl in the world," he enters slowly. He moves to the edge of the lighted half, looking about him, still singing. Finally he turns away and is beginning to move, when* JOAN *joins in the song softly from her hiding-place. Very quickly he closes the curtains at the archway, but as he turns his back* JOAN *jumps up and turns off the switch of the standard lamp down* L., *and returns to her hiding-place. The stage is now in darkness except for the blue sky at the window.)*

ROBIN. All right, Joan Helford. Where are you, Joan Helford, where are you ?

(She is heard to laugh in the darkness. She rises and crosses below the ottoman to down R., *then runs up to the window and jumps on to the window-seat, pulling the* L. *curtain over her.)*

You can't escape, Joan Helford, you can't escape   No, no.

(As he follows her round.) No, no. No escape for little Joan. No escape.

(As he is saying this, in a mock threatening tone, he is crossing to the window, and now he pulls aside the L. curtain—in one quick movement—and a vague moonlight comes into the room, just lighting up the right-hand half of it. He finds her and, taking hold of both her hands, slowly pulls her off the window-seat to the ground. They are silhouetted against the blue sky ; ROBIN R., JOAN L. *First he holds her at arms' length by both hands, but then he slowly pulls her towards him, and then when he lets go of her hands, she puts her arms round his neck . he puts his arms round her, and they kiss, not at too great a length.)*

JOAN *(really moved)*. Oh—Robin !

ROBIN *(mocking—but nicely)*. Oh—Joan !

JOAN *(shyly)*. I suppose—you've been—doing this—to dozens of girls ?

ROBIN *(still light)*. Yes, Joan, dozens.

JOAN *(looking up at him)*. I thought so.

ROBIN *(a trifle unsteadily)*. Like that, Joan. But not— like this—— *(Now he kisses her with more ardour.)*

JOAN *(deeply moved, but still shy)*. Robin—you *are* sweet——

ROBIN *(after a pause)*. You know, Joan, although it's not so very long since I saw you last, I couldn't believe my eyes to-night—you looked so stunning——

JOAN *(sincerely, shyly)*. It was because I'd just heard that you'd come back, Robin.

ROBIN *(who does)*. I don't believe it.

JOAN *(sincerely)*. Yes, it's true—honestly—I don't suppose you've ever thought about me, have you ?

ROBIN *(who hasn't)*. Yes, I have. Hundreds of times.

JOAN. I have about you too.

ROBIN *(kissing her)*. Joan, you're a darling !

JOAN *(after a pause, whispering)*. Do you remember that morning you went away so early—a year ago ?

ROBIN. Yes. But you weren't there. Only Mother and Hazel and Kay.

JOAN. I was there too, but I didn't let any of you see me——

ROBIN *(genuinely surprised)*. You got up at that filthy hour just to see me go ?

JOAN *(simply)*. Yes, of course. Oh—it was awful—trying to hide and trying not to cry, all at the same time——

ROBIN *(still surprised, and moved)*. But, Joan, I'd no idea——

JOAN *(very shyly)*. I didn't mean to give myself away——

ROBIN *(embracing her)*. But, Joan—oh, gosh !—it's mar-vellous——

JOAN. You don't love me ?

ROBIN *(now sure he does)*. Of course I do. *(He kisses her again.*)   Golly, this is great !   Joan, we'll have a scrumptious time !

JOAN (*solemnly*).   Yes, let's.   But, Robin—it's terribly *serious*, y'know.

ROBIN.   Oh—yes—don't think I don't feel that too.   But that's no reason why we shouldn't enjoy ourselves, is it ?

JOAN (*crying out*).   No, no, no.   Let's be happy for ever and ever——

(*They embrace fervently, silhouetted against the moonlit window. CAROL enters suddenly and switches on the chandelier from the switch below the arch and sees them.*)

CAROL (*with a sort of cheerful disgust*).   I thought so !   (*Turning to call to the people off.*)   They're in here—courting !   I knew there was a catch in this hide-and-seek.   (*She hooks back the curtains at the arch.*)

(ROBIN and JOAN *have sprung apart, but still hold hands.* MADGE *and* GERALD *enter.* MADGE *goes towards the window ;* GERALD, *who has the copy of* " The Nation," *moves down to* R. *of the ottoman.* MADGE *is rather excited—and rather untidy too, as if she had been hiding in some difficult place.*)

ROBIN (*grinning*).   Sorry !   Shall we start again ?
MADGE.   No, thank you, Robin.
CAROL.   You'd better explain to Mother.   I'm going to make tea.

(*She goes off to* R.   ROBIN *and* JOAN *look at each other, then go out.* GERALD *watches* MADGE, *who now goes behind the chesterfield and down* L. *to switch on the standard lamp.*)

GERALD (*down* R.).   Well, Madge, it sounds all right.   And I know Lord Robert Cecil's a fine chap.   But I don't quite see where I come into it.

MADGE (*crossing to* L. *of the ottoman*).   Because in a few weeks' time there'll be a branch of this League of Nations Union here in Newlingham.   It's no use my doing much about it—though I'll join, of course—because I'll be away.   But you could be organizing secretary or something, Gerald.

GERALD.   Don't know that I'd be much good.

MADGE (*kneeling on the* L. *seat of the ottoman, facing him*). You'd be perfect.   You understand business.   You know how to handle people.   You'd make a good public speaker.   Oh, Gerald —you're maddening !

GERALD (*smiling, not without affection*).   Why, Madge ?   What have I done now ?

MADGE.   We're friends, aren't we ?

GERALD.   I consider you one of my very best friends, Madge, and I hope I'm not flattering myself.

MADGE (*warmly*). Of course not.

GERALD (*smiling*). Good ! So ?

MADGE. You're not doing enough, Gerald.

GERALD (*mildly*). I'm kept pretty busy, y'know.

MADGE. Yes, I don't mean you're lazy—though I'm not sure that you aren't a bit, y'know, Gerald—I mean you're not doing enough with yourself. I could be *tremendously* proud of you, Gerald.

GERALD. That's—almost overwhelming—coming from you, Madge.

MADGE. Why from me ?

GERALD (*sitting on the* R. *seat of the ottoman*). Because I know very well that you've got a very good brain and are a most critical young woman. Rather frightening.

MADGE (*sitting back on her heels—rather more feminine here*). Nonsense ! You don't mean that. I'd much rather you didn't, y'know.

GERALD. All right, I don't. As a matter of fact, I'm very fond of you, Madge, but don't often get a chance of showing you that I am.

MADGE (*lighting up at this*). I've always been fond of you, Gerald, and that's why I say I could be tremendously proud of you.

(*She takes his copy of " The Nation " from him.*)

(*With more breadth and sweep and real warm enthusiasm.*) We're going to build up a new world now. This horrible War was probably necessary because it was a great bonfire on which we threw all the old nasty rubbish of the world. Civilization can really begin—at last. People have learned their lesson——

GERALD (*dubiously*). I hope so.

MADGE (*rising and crossing* L. *to below the chesterfield*). Oh—Gerald—don't be so pessimistic, so cynical——

GERALD. Sorry, but a lawyer—even a young one—sees a lot of human nature in his office. There's a procession of people with their quarrels and grievances. And sometimes I wonder how much people are capable of learning. (*He crosses below the ottoman to* C.)

MADGE. That's because you have to deal with some of the stupidest. But *the* people—all over the world—have learned their lesson. You'll see. No more piling up armaments. No more wars. No more hate and intolerance and violence. (*Kneeling in the* R. *corner of the chesterfield.*) Oh—Gerald—I believe that when we look back—in twenty years' time—we'll be staggered at the progress that's been made. Because things happen quickly now——

GERALD (*going up to* R. *of her at* R. *end of the chesterfield*). That's true enough.

MADGE (*begins to orate a little, sincerely*). And so is all the rest. Under the League, we'll build up a new commonwealth of all the nations, so that they can live at peace for ever. And Imperialism will go. And so in the end, of course, will Capitalism. There'll be no more booms and slumps and panics and strikes and lock-outs, because the people themselves, led by the best brains in their countries, will possess both the political and economic power. There'll be Socialism at last, a free, prosperous, happy people, all enjoying equal opportunities, living at peace with the whole world. (*She quotes with great fervour and sincerity.*)

Bring me my Bow of burning gold :
Bring me my Arrows of desire :
Bring me my Spear : O clouds unfold !
Bring me my Chariot of fire.

I will not cease from Mental Fight,
Nor shall my Sword sleep in my hand
Till we have built Jerusalem
In England's green and pleasant Land . . .

GERALD (*genuinely moved by her fervour*). Madge—I—I hardly recognize you—you're——
MADGE (*taking his hands—warmly, happily*). This is the real me. Oh !—Gerald—in this New World we're going to build up now, men and women won't play a silly little game of cross-purposes any longer. They'll go forward together—sharing everything. (*Rising to her feet on the chesterfield.*) Oh, Gerald, if you . . .

(MRS. CONWAY *enters with* HAZEL, *who is carrying a tea-tray.* MADGE *breaks off, looking rather untidy.* GERALD, *who has been genuinely dominated by her, looks round, recovering himself.*)

MRS. CONWAY (*at the arch, with maddening maternal briskness*). Madge dear !

(MADGE *gets off the chesterfield, and drops down* L. GERALD *drops down to below* L. *corner of the ottoman.* HAZEL *is putting the tea-tray on the table up* R. MRS. CONWAY *crosses above the ottoman to* R. *of* MADGE L.C.)

Your hair's all over the place, you've made your nose all shiny, you're horribly untidy, and I'm sure you're in the middle of a Socialist speech that must be boring poor Gerald.

(*The generous mood is shattered.* MADGE *might have been hit in the face. She looks at her mother, then looks quickly at* GERALD, *reads something in his face—a sort of withdrawal from her—that is somehow final, and then in complete silence walks straight out of the room.*)

(*Lightly, but knowing what has happened.*) Poor Madge !

HAZEL (*coming down to* MRS. CONWAY—*with sudden reproach*).
Mother !

MRS. CONWAY (*with wide innocence*). What, Hazel ?

HAZEL (*significantly*). You know ! (*She goes to the table
up* R. *again.*)

GERALD. I think—I'd better be going.

MRS. CONWAY (*easily*). Oh—no, Gerald, don't go. Kay and
Carol are making some tea and we're all going to be nice and
cosy together in here.

GERALD. I fancy it's rather late, though. (*He glances at
his watch.*) After eleven. I *must* go. I've an early appoint-
ment in the morning, and one or two things to look through
before I turn in to-night. So—— (*With slight smile.*)

(KAY *enters with folding legs for the tea-tray and crosses above
the ottoman to below* R. *end of the chesterfield between* GERALD
and MRS. CONWAY. *She opens the legs and places them below*
R. *end of the chesterfield.* HAZEL *exits.*)

Good night, Kay. Thank you for a very nice party. And
now that you're properly grown-up, I hope you'll be happy.

KAY (*with a slight smile*). Thank you, Gerald. Do you think
I will ?

GERALD (*his smile suddenly vanishing*). I don't know, Kay.
I really don't know.

(*He smiles and shakes hands with* KAY, *then turns to* MRS. CONWAY.)

MRS. CONWAY. No. I'll see you out, Gerald.

(*They go above the ottoman and off. In the hall they pass* HAZEL,
who is re-entering with two plates of cakes. GERALD *and* HAZEL
exchange " Good nights.")

HAZEL (*thoughtfully, as she crosses to put the plates on the table
behind the chesterfield*). I've always thought it must be much
more *fun* being a girl than being a man. (*She passes on behind
the chesterfield and sits on the* L. *arm.*)

KAY (*fetching the tea-tray from the table up* R. *and putting it
on the legs below the chesterfield*). I'm never sure. Sometimes
men seem quite hopelessly dull, like creatures made out of wood.
And then at other times they seem to have all the fun.

HAZEL (*very seriously for her*). Kay, just now—this very
minute—I wish I wasn't a girl. I'd like to be a man—one of
those men with red faces and loud voices who just don't care
what anybody says about them.

KAY (*laughingly*). Perhaps they do, though.

HAZEL. I'd like to be one of those who don't.

KAY. Why all this ?

(HAZEL *shakes her head.* CAROL *and* ALAN *enter ;* CAROL *with
a large earthenware teapot,* ALAN *with a kettle of hot water.*)

CAROL (*crossing and putting the teapot on the tea-tray*). Alan says he wants to go to bed.

KAY. Oh—no, Alan. Don't spoil it.

ALAN (*crossing below* CAROL *to* L. *to put the kettle on the anthracite stove*). How could I ?

KAY. By going to bed. It's my birthday, and you're not to go until I give you leave.

CAROL (*going to* ALAN, *who is standing with his back to the fire— severely*). Quite right, Kay. (*To* ALAN.) And that's because we're very, very fond of you, Alan, though you are such a chump. (*As he takes his pipe from his pocket and puts it in his mouth.*) You must smoke your pipe too—for cosiness. (*Generally.*) Robin and Joan are courting in the dining-room now. (*Jumping on to the chesterfield and sitting on the back of it in the* R. *corner.*) I can see they're going to be an awful nuisance.

KAY (R. *of the chesterfield*). If you had to fall in love with somebody, would you like it to be at home or somewhere else ?

HAZEL (*seated on the* L. *arm of the chesterfield*). Somewhere else. Too ordinary at home. On a yacht or the terrace at Monte Carlo or a Pacific island. Marvellous !

CAROL. That would be using up too many things at once. Greedy stuff !

HAZEL (*coolly*). I am greedy.

CAROL. I should think so. (*To the other two.*) Yesterday morning she was in the bath, reading *Greenmantle* and eating nut-milk chocolate.

KAY (*who has been thinking, moving to above the ottoman and kneeling on the upstage seat of it*). No, it wouldn't be too ordinary, falling in love at home here. It would be best, I think. Suppose you were suddenly unhappy. It would be awful to be desperately unhappy and in love, miles away, in a strange house. . . . (*She suddenly stops and shivers.*)

CAROL. Kay, what's the matter ?

KAY. Nothing. (*She abruptly turns away up to the window and closes the curtains.*)

CAROL (*solemnly*). Then it must have been a goose walking over your grave.

(HAZEL *looks at* KAY—*as the other two do—then raises her eyebrows at* CAROL, *who shakes her head sternly.* MRS. CONWAY *enters and looks cheerful at the sight of the tea.*)

MRS. CONWAY (*cheerfully, as she crosses to sit at* R. *end of the chesterfield*). Now then, let's have some tea and be nice and cosy together. Where's Robin ?

HAZEL. Spooning with Joan in the dining-room.

MRS. CONWAY. Oh !—hasn't Joan gone yet ? I really think she might leave us to ourselves now. After all, it's the first time we've all been together in this house for—how long ? It

must be at least three years. I'll pour out. Come on, Kay.
What's the matter ?

CAROL (*in a tremendous whisper, seriously*). Sh ! It's a *mood*.

(*But* KAY *returns and sits on the* L. *seat of the ottoman, looking
rather strained. Her Mother looks at her carefully, smiling.*
KAY *manages an answering smile.*)

MRS. CONWAY. That's better, darling. What a funny child
you are, aren't you ?

KAY. Not really, Mother. Where's Madge ?

ALAN. She went upstairs.

MRS. CONWAY. Go up, dear, and tell her we're all in here,
with some tea, and ask her—very nicely, dear, specially from
me—to come down.

HAZEL (*muttering*). I'll bet she doesn't.

(ALAN *goes.* MRS. CONWAY *begins pouring out tea.*)

MRS. CONWAY. This is just like old times, isn't it ? And we
seem to have waited so long. I ought to tell fortunes again—
to-night.

HAZEL (*eagerly*). Oh—yes—Mother, do.

KAY (*rather sharply*). No.

MRS. CONWAY. Kay ! Really !

KAY. Sorry, Mother. Somehow, I hated the idea of you
messing about with those cards to-night. I never did like it much.

CAROL (*who has got off the chesterfield and now hands* KAY *a
cup of tea—solemnly*). I believe only the Bad Things come true.
(*She perches herself on the* R. *corner back of the chesterfield again.*)

MRS. CONWAY. Certainly not. I clearly saw Madge's Girton
scholarship, you remember. I said she was going to get one,
didn't I ? And I always said Robin and Alan would come
back. I saw it every time in the cards.

(*Enter* JOAN *and* ROBIN. CAROL *coughs mockingly.* JOAN
comes to R. *of* MRS. CONWAY. ROBIN *lingers above.*)

JOAN. I—I think I ought to go now, Mrs. Conway. (*To*
KAY, *impulsively.*) Thank you so much, Kay, it's been the
loveliest party there ever was. (*She suddenly kisses her with
great affection, then goes to* MRS. CONWAY, *who is now standing.*)
I really have had a marvellous time, Mrs. Conway.

(*She is standing close to* MRS. CONWAY *now. The latter looks
quite searchingly at her.* JOAN *meets her look quite bravely,
though a little shaky.* ROBIN *drops down* R. *of* JOAN, *puts his
arm round her and they ·stand facing* MRS. CONWAY.)

ROBIN. Well, Mother ?

MRS. CONWAY *looks at him, then at* JOAN, *and suddenly smiles.*
JOAN *smiles back.*)

MRS. CONWAY. Are you two children *serious* ?
ROBIN (*boisterously*). Of course we are.
MRS. CONWAY. Joan ?
JOAN (*very solemnly, nervously*). Yes.
MRS. CONWAY (*with an air of capitulation*). I think you'd better have a cup of tea, hadn't you ?

(JOAN *flings her arms round* MRS. CONWAY *and kisses her excitedly.*)

JOAN. I'm so happy.
CAROL (*loudly and cheerfully*). What did I tell you, Kay—courting everywhere ! (*Jumping about by* R. *end of the chesterfield.*) Tea. Tea. Tea.

(JOAN *crosses and sits in the chair below the fire* L. ROBIN *sits on the low footstool by the fire, with his back to the stove and his legs stretched out across the hearth-rug. The cups of tea are passed round.* ALAN *re-enters.*)

ALAN. Madge says she's too tired, Mother. (*He sits on the* R. *seat of the ottoman.*)

(CAROL *gives* ALAN *a cup of tea and returns to sit on the* R. *back corner of the chesterfield.*)

MRS. CONWAY. Well, I think we can get on very nicely without Madge. Kay ought to read us some of the new novel she's writing——

(*Exclamations of agreement and approval from* JOAN *and* ROBIN, *and a groan from* HAZEL.)

KAY (*in horror*). I couldn't possibly, Mother.
MRS. CONWAY. I can't see why not. You always expect me to be ready to sing for you.
KAY. That's different.
MRS. CONWAY (*mostly to* ROBIN *and* JOAN). Kay's always so solemn and secretive about her writing—as if she were ashamed of it.
KAY (*bravely*). I am—in a way. I know it's not good enough yet. Most of it's stupid, stupid, *stupid*.
CAROL (*indignantly*). It isn't, Kay.
KAY. Yes, it is, angel. But it won't always be. It *must* come right if I only keep on trying. And then—you'll see.
JOAN. Is that what you want to do, Kay ? Just to write novels and things ?
KAY. Yes. But there's nothing in simply writing. The point is to be *good*—to be sensitive and sincere. Hardly anybody's both, especially women who write. But I'm going to try and be. And whatever happens, I'm never, *never* going to write except what I want to write, what I feel is true to me,

deep down. I won't write just to please silly people or just to make money. I'll——

(*But she suddenly breaks off. The rest wait and stare.*)

ALAN (*encouragingly*). Go on, Kay.

KAY (*confusedly, dejectedly*). No—Alan—I'd finished really —or if I was going to say something else, I've forgotten what it was—nothing much——

MRS. CONWAY (*not too concernedly*). You're sure you're not over-tired, Kay ?

KAY (*hastily*). No, Mother. Really.

MRS. CONWAY. I wonder what will have happened to you, Hazel, when Kay's a famous novelist ? Perhaps one of your majors and captains will come back for you soon. (*She puts her arm round* HAZEL, *who cuddles close to her.*)

HAZEL (*calmly*). They needn't. In fact, I'd rather none of them didn't.

ROBIN (*teasingly*). Thinks she can do much better than them.

HAZEL (*calmly*). I know I can. I shall marry a tall, rather good-looking man about five or six years older than I am, and he'll have plenty of money and be very fond of travel, and we'll go all over the world together but have a house in London.

MRS. CONWAY. And what about poor Newlingham ?

HAZEL. Mother, I couldn't possibly spend the rest of my life here. I'd die. But you shall come and stay with us in London, and we'll give parties so that people can come and stare at my sister, Kay Conway, the famous novelist.

ROBIN (*boisterously*). And what about your brother, Robin, the famous—oh ! famous something-or-other, you bet your life.

JOAN (*rather teasingly*). You don't know what you're going to do yet, Robin.

ROBIN (*grandly*). Well, give me a chance. I've only been out of the Air Force about twelve hours. But—by jingo— I'm going to do *something*. And none of this starting-at-the-bottom-of-the-ladder, pushing-a-pen-in-a-corner business either. This is a time when young men get a chance, and I'm going to take it. You watch.

MRS. CONWAY (*with mock alarm, though with underlying seriousness*). Don't tell me you're going to run away from Newlingham too !

ROBIN (*grandly*). Oh—well—I don't know about that yet, Mother. I might make a start here—there's some money in the place, thanks to some jolly rotten profiteering, and we're pretty well known here, so that would help—but I don't guarantee to take root in Newlingham, no fear ! Don't be surprised, Hazel, if I'm in London before you. Or even before you, Kay. *And* making plenty of money. (*To* HAZEL.) Perhaps more than this tall, good-looking chap of yours will be making·

CAROL (*sharply, pointing*). Hazel will always have plenty of money.

MRS. CONWAY (*amused*). How do you know, Carol ?

CAROL. I just do. It came over me suddenly then.

MRS. CONWAY (*still amused*). Well now ! I thought I was the prophetic one of the family. (*Caressing her.*) I suppose it wouldn't be fair if I sent my rival to bed.

CAROL. I should jolly well think it wouldn't. And I'll tell you another thing. (*She points suddenly to* ALAN.) Alan's the happy one.

ROBIN. Good old Alan !

ALAN. I—rather think—you're wrong there, y'know, Carol.

CAROL. I'm not. I *know*.

MRS. CONWAY. Now, I'm not going to have this. I'm the one who *knows* in this family. Now wait a minute.

(JOAN *puts a cushion on the floor in front of her chair and sits on it.* MRS. CONWAY *covers her eyes with her hands for a moment.*)

(*Playfully, half seriously.*) Yes. I see Robin dashing about, making lots of money and becoming very important and helping some of you others. And a very devoted young wife by his side. And Hazel, of course, being very grand. And her husband *is* tall and *quite* good-looking, nearly as good-looking as she thinks he is. I believe he comes into a title.

ROBIN. Snob !

MRS. CONWAY. I don't see Madge marrying, but then she'll be headmistress of a big school quite soon, and then she'll be-come one of these women who are on all sorts of committees and have to go up to London to give evidence, and so becomes happy and grand that way.

ROBIN. I'll bet she will too, good old Madge !

MRS. CONWAY (*gaily*). I'll go and stay with her sometimes—*very* important, the headmistress's mother—and the other mistresses will be invited in to dine and will listen *very* respect-fully while I tell them about my other children——

JOAN (*happily, admiringly*). Oh—Mrs. Conway—I can just imagine that. You'll have a *marvellous* time.

MRS. CONWAY (*same vein*). Then there's Carol. Well, of course, Carol will be here with me for years yet——

CAROL (*excitedly*). I don't know about that. I haven't exactly decided *what* to do yet, there are so many things to do.

JOAN. Oh—Carol—I think you could go on the stage.

CAROL (*with growing excitement*). Yes, I could, of course, and I've often thought of it. But I shouldn't want to be on the stage *all* the time—and when I wasn't playing a part, I'd like to be painting pictures—just for myself, y'know—daubing like mad—with lots and lots and lots of the very brightest paint—tubes and tubes of vermilion and royal blue and emerald green and gamboge and cobalt and Chinese White   And then making all kinds of weird dresses for myself.   And scarlet cloaks.   And black crêpe-de-chine gowns with orange dragons all over them.   And cooking !   (*Leaning forward on the arm of the chesterfield.*)   Yes, doing sausages and gingerbread and pancakes.   And sitting on the top of mountains and going down rivers in canoes.   And making friends with all sorts of people. And I'd share a flat or a little house with Kay in London, and Alan would come to stay with us and smoke his pipe, and we'd talk about books and laugh at *ridiculous* people, and then go to foreign countries——

ROBIN (*calling through*).   Hoy, hoy, steady !

MRS. CONWAY (*affectionately amused*).   How are you going to *begin* doing all that, you ridiculous child ?

CAROL (*excitedly*).   I'd get it all in somehow.   The point is —to live.   Never mind about money and positions and husbands with titles and rubbish—I'm *going to live.*

MRS. CONWAY.   All right, darling.   (*She has now caught the infection.*)   But wherever you were, all of you, and whatever you were doing, you'd all come back here, sometimes, wouldn't you ?   I'd come and see you, but you'd all come and see me too, all together, perhaps with wives and husbands and lovely children of your own, not being rich and famous or anything, but just being yourselves, as you are now, enjoying our silly old jokes, sometimes playing the same silly old games, all one big happy family.   I can see us all here again——

KAY (*rising with a terrible cry*).   Don't !   Don't ! !

(*They stare in silent consternation.*)

MRS. CONWAY.   But what is it, Kay ?

(KAY, *sobbing, shakes her head.   The others exchange puzzled glances, but* CAROL *comes down to* L. *of her, all tenderness, and puts her arms round her.*)

CAROL (*with the solemnity of a child*).   I won't bother with any of those things, Kay, really I won't.   I'll come and look after you wherever you go.   I won't leave you ever if you don't want me to.   I'll look after you, darling.

(KAY *stops crying.   She looks—half-smiling—at* CAROL *in a puzzled, wistful fashion.   * CAROL *backs and sits again on the* R. *arm of the chesterfield.*)

MRS. CONWAY (*reproachful but affectionate*).   Really, Kay ! What's the matter ?

(KAY *shakes her head, then comes forward, looking very earnestly at* ALAN.)

KAY (*struggling with some thought*). Alan . . . please tell
me . . . I can't bear it . . . and there's something . . . something . . . you could tell me . . .

ALAN (*troubled, bewildered*). I'm sorry, Kay. I don't understand. What is it ?

KAY (*going on, same vein*). Something you know—that
would make it different—not so hard to bear. Don't you know
yet ?

ALAN (*stammering*). No—I don't—understand——

KAY. Oh—hurry, hurry, Alan—and then—tell me and comfort me. Something—of Blake's—came into it—— (*She looks
hard at him, then struggling, remembers, saying brokenly.*)

> Joy . . . and woe . . . are woven fine,
> A clothing for the . . . soul divine . . .

I used to know that verse too. What was it at the end ? (*She
remembers, as before.*)

> And, when this . . . we rightly know,
> Safely through the world we go.

Safely . . . through the world we go. . . . (*She looks like
breaking down again, but recovers herself.*)

MRS. CONWAY (*after a pause, almost a whisper*). Over-excite-
ment. I might have known. (*She rises to* L. *of* KAY *and speaks
cheerfully, but firmly.*) Kay darling, all this birthday excitement's been too much. You'd better go to bed now, dear,
and Carol shall bring you some hot milk. Perhaps an aspirin
too, eh ?

(KAY, *recovering from her grief, shakes her head.*)

You're all right now, aren't you, darling ?

KAY (*in muffled voice*). Yes, Mother, I'm all right. (*But she
turns and goes to the window, parting the curtains a little and
looking out towards* L.)

MRS. CONWAY. I know what might help, it did once before.
Robin, come with me.

JOAN (*rising—rather helplessly*). I ought to go, oughtn't I ?

MRS. CONWAY. No, stay a few minutes, Joan. Robin !

(MRS. CONWAY *and* ROBIN *go out.* HAZEL *moves along towards
the* R. *end of the chesterfield so that* JOAN *may sit beside her at*
L. *end.*)

CAROL (*whispering*). She's going to sing, and I know what
it will be.

(CAROL *switches off all the lights—chandelier and standard lamp—
at the switches below the archway and returns to sit perched up
on the* R. *arm of the chesterfield. The three girls on the chesterfield*

*form a ghostly group, caught by the light from the arch. KAY
has the curtains parted sufficiently for the moonlight to light her.*
    MRS. CONWAY *has started singing " Wiegenlied " softly as
the lights are switched out.*
    ALAN *rises and goes up to behind* KAY, R. *of her, so that the
moonlight catches him over her shoulder.)*

ALAN (*very quietly*). Kay.
KAY (*very quietly*). Yes, Alan ?
ALAN (*very quietly*). There will be—something—I can tell
you—one day. I'll try—to be wise—I promise.

*The song swells and the lights begin to fade. The light on the three
girls goes first ; the moonlight on* KAY *and* ALAN *fades gradually
and is out by the last note of the song, when*

The CURTAIN falls.

PROPERTY PLOT

ACT I

Set Stage as Photograph.
The following are the essential properties :

On Stage.

Copy of " The Nation " on table behind chesterfield.
Safety-pins on table up R.
Box of chocolates on table up ʙ
Cigarette-box with cigarettes, matcnes and ashtray on table up ᴍ.
2 cushions on chesterfield.
1 cushion on chair down L.
Pad of paper and pencil in drawer of desk ʀ.

Off Stage.

Old clothes, including Norfolk coat, and hats for Hazel.
Cigar-box filled with old false moustaches and beards, false noses, monocles and spectacles, etc., for Carol.
Old lady's felt hat containing small black fan, red rose and Spanish comb for Carol.
Sheet of paper and pencil for Kay.
Glass of claret cup for Mrs. Conway.
Small parcel containing silk scarf for Robin.
Tray with sandwiches, cake, glass and bottle of beer for Mrs. Conway.

Personal.

Pipe, pouch and matches for Alan.

ACT II

Set Stage as Photograph.
The following are the essential properties :

On Stage.

Ashtray on table c.
Cigarette-box with cigarettes, matches, ashtray, on mantelpiece.
Envelope in L. drawer of table.
Ink-bottle on desk up R.
Cigarette-box with cigarettes, matches, ashtray, on small table up L.
Book on chesterfield.

Off Stage.

Tray with port, whisky, soda and glasses for Alan.
Brief-case with papers for Gerald.
Evening paper for Ernest.
Small parcel containing cheap handbag for Alan.
Copy of " Time and Tide " for Madge.
Small diamond brooch in case in handbag for Mrs. Conway.

Personal.

Fountain-pen for Madge.
Cigar for Ernest.
Pipe, pouch and matches for Alan.

ACT III

Set Stage as at end of Act I.
The following properties are essential :

On Stage.
  Copy of " The Nation " on chair above desk.

Off Stage.
  Plate with piece of rich creamy cake for HAZEL.
  Copy of " The Nation " for GERALD.
  Tea-tray with milk, sugar, cups, saucers, spoons, etc., for HAZEL.
  Legs of tea-tray for KAY.
  2 plates of cakes for HAZEL.
  Large earthenware tea-pot for CAROL.
  Kettle of hot water for ALAN.

Personal.
  Pipe, pouch and matches for ALAN.

MADE AND PRINTED IN GREAT BRITAIN BY
LATIMER TREND & COMPANY LTD PLYMOUTH

MADE IN ENGLAND

Breinigsville, PA USA
09 September 2010

245026BV00006B/4/P